Victoria

Thank you for your guidance
and for being a friend.

Adewale

CREATIVE ENDEAVOUR FOR THE LOGICAL MIND

How to Go from Engineer to Entrepreneur

Adewale J. Lawal

CREATIVE ENDEAVOUR OF THE LOGICAL MIND
www. creativelogicalmind.com

Copyright © 2018 Adewale J. Lawal

ISBN-13: 978-1729761304
ISBN-10: 1729761305

All rights reserved. No portion of this book may be reproduced mechanically, electronically, or by any other means, including photocopying, without permission of the publisher or author except in the case of brief quotations embodied in critical articles and reviews. It is illegal to copy this book, post it to a website, or distribute it by any other means without permission from the publisher or author.

Limits of Liability and Disclaimer of Warranty
The author and publisher shall not be liable for your misuse of the enclosed material. This book is strictly for informational and educational purposes only.

Warning – Disclaimer
The purpose of this book is to educate and entertain. The author does not guarantee that anyone following these techniques, suggestions, tips, ideas, or strategies will become successful. The author and/or publisher shall have neither liability nor responsibility to anyone with respect to any loss or damage caused, or alleged to be caused, directly or indirectly by the information contained in this book.

Medical Disclaimer
The medical or health information in this book is provided as an information resource only, and is not to be used or relied on for any diagnostic or treatment purposes. This information is not intended to be patient education, does not create any patient-physician relationship, and should not be used as a substitute for professional diagnosis and treatment.

Publisher
10-10-10 Publishing
Markham, ON
Canada

Printed in Canada and the United States of America

Table of Contents

Dedication	v
About the Author	ix
Foreword	xi
Chapter 1: Engineer to Entrepreneur	**1**
School	1
University	5
The Surrey Thing	5
Continuous Tinkering	11
Lessons Learnt from 1st Job	12
Corporate Life	14
The Transition	17
Chapter 2: Create the Right Mindset, and Know your Why	**21**
Creating the Correct Mindset	21
Having a Millionaire Mindset	23
The Two Mindsets	25
Know Your Why	27
Chapter 3: Getting Started	**31**
Choose Your Niche	31
Invest in Your Education	35
Learn About the Industry	37
Set Your Budget	39
Test, Fail, Test, Fail, Test, Kaboom	41

Chapter 4: Getting a Mentor — 43
Importance of Finding a Mentor — 43
What They Can Do For You — 44
A Good Mentor — 46
Finding Your Mentor in Your Niche — 49

Chapter 5: Your Customers — 51
Put Yourself in Their Shoes — 52
Build Relationships — 53
Tell Them Your Story — 55
Thank Your Customer — 57
Provide Especially Great Customer Service — 58

Chapter 6: Strategy — 61
Never Try to Sell at the Lowest Price — 61
Apply the 80/20 Rule — 62
Sell to Hot Marketplaces — 64
Harness Repeat Behaviour — 65
Think Win-Win — 67

Chapter 7: Traffic — 69
What is Traffic? — 69
Free Traffic Generation — 70
Paid Traffic Generation Strategies — 74
Paid Traffic vs Free Traffic — 76
Traffic You Own – Subscribers — 78
Social Media Advertising

Chapter 8: Build Your List   **85**
The Importance of Having a List   85
Choosing the Right Software   86
The Honey Pot   88
Writing Emails and Follow-up   89

Chapter 9: Leads and Conversions   **93**
Leads   93
Conversions   95
Tactics to Increase Conversions   96
Planning and Documentation   98
Creatives   100

Chapter 10: Accomplishing Your Goals   **103**
Milestones and Goals   103
WIN, WIN, WIN   105
Who Are You?   107
Mind Your Own Business   109

Dedication

Dedicated to my father, Admiral Adekunle S. Lawal, (NN) B.Sc.Eng., M.Sc.Eng., CMarEng., FIMarEng., FSS. PSC.: son, brother, husband, father, friend, inspiration (1934–1980).

Dear Daddy,
I dedicate this book to you. I am the man that I am today because you and mummy always taught me how to stay positive, work hard, and be an honest, helpful, and selfless human being. I miss you so much.

He Is Gone

You can shed tears that he is gone, or you can smile because he has lived. You can close your eyes and pray that he will come back, or you can open your eyes and see all that he has left. Your heart can be empty because you can't see him, or you can be full of the love that you shared. You can turn your back on tomorrow and live yesterday, or you can be happy for tomorrow because of yesterday. You can remember him and only that he is gone, or you can cherish his memory and let it live on. You can cry and close your mind, be empty and turn your back, or you can do what he would want: smile, open your eyes, love, and go on.

– David Harkins

Acknowledgements

I would like to thank my loving wife, who has supported me in sickness and in health for many years without complaint. She has driven me to be the best I could be. She is now part of my soul.

I thank you, my mother, for raising me the way you did. Thank you for the morals you instilled in me, and the endless love, guidance, patience, and admiration you have given me. I would not be the person I am today without you.

Also, my sisters and brothers need to mentioned, as they have also supported me and advised me. A special acknowledgement goes out to my brother, Gbenga, without whom I might not be here. Thank you for being my friend and donor.

I must thank the congregation of Ely Cathedral, especially Linda, Joan, Angela, and Mary. Thank you for your kindness, love, and support in the darkest hours, and a big thank you to Canon Victoria Johnson, and Dean, the Very Reverend Mark Bonney, for their help and support when I was sick.

Creative Endeavour for the Logical Mind

A big acknowledgement and thank you to my friends, Suzanne, Paul, Paul, Carol, Kevin, Neal, Kevin, and Steve, for just being there when I needed to talk to someone or ask for advice. You are the best friends anyone could ask for.

I thank Shaqir Hussyin, who taught me about the marketing world and how to get started. He is my guru and mentor in this world.

I thank Mr. Raymond Aaron, a *New York Times* top-10 bestselling author, who has provided me with a wealth of knowledge, and is a friend who has advised me in so many positive ways.

There are many more people I could thank, but time, space, and modesty compel me to stop here.

About the Author

Adewale Lawal, author of Creative Endeavour for the Logical Mind, is a Chartered Mechanical Engineer and Masters Graduate of Surrey University. He carved out a career in manufacturing before starting his own successful business as a Manufacturing Consultant, providing incisive and expert advice to the world's leading blue-chip companies.

Following a prolonged period of ill health, all this changed for Adewale. He decided to explore ways to build an online business, soon finding himself in the realms of online marketing, and discovered a whole new discipline and language, at the polar opposite of the more familiar engineering world. Realising there was a method, process, and system in this new world, the intricacies of online marketing began to gradually unravel. Recognising how sophisticated building an online business can be, Adewale invested heavily in his education, and committed to learning and masterminding from the best in the industry, who have achieved success in this field.

Adewale lives in Cambridgeshire with his wife, Julie, who shares his new-found passion for marketing, building online businesses, and helping other people make the same transformational life changes.

You can contact him on www.adewalelawal.com for more information and to book a consultation.

Foreword

Are you living the life you've always wanted to live?

Imagine for a moment how it would feel to enjoy a life of financial freedom, one that's unconstrained by time. Do you think this would open up more choices for you and your family that you have right now?

Do you fantasize about taking more vacations with your loved ones? Are you planning for retirement, worrying that you will be unable to live comfortably with only your pension? Do you wish your legacy for your loved ones could be more?

Author Adewale Lawal is a chartered mechanical engineer, who for many years lived the life of a consultant to blue chip companies all over the world. After being struck by ill health and overcoming adversity, Adewale made the decision to change his lifestyle and become an entrepreneur in the field of online business education, which allowed him the freedom to spend more time with his loved ones.

Creative Endeavour for the Logical Mind documents his journey, and gives you the steps to take in order to face the challenges of doing business online. No matter what your

Creative Endeavour for the Logical Mind

current situation is, this book will show you how to create massive change in your life and finances, so that you too can tap into joyfulness.

Raymond Aaron
New York Times Bestselling Author

Chapter 1

Engineer to Entrepreneur

The main quote that impacted me while growing up was:

"I'm trying to find out in life where yours ends and mine begins. You live in me, and I in you. I am proud to be your son and will always and forever love and honour you. I am so proud and honoured to be your son." – from Ken Sara Wiwa's son.

This is because he grew up without his father for much of his life (he was killed for political reasons), much like I grew up without my father, who unfortunately died at an early age. In life, we all go through challenges, but it is what we do to overcome these challenges that makes us who we are.

School

My family tended to travel around the globe to exotic countries surrounding the Arabian, Red, and Mediterranean Seas, after I was born, as my father was in the Navy. Finally, settling back in Nigeria, I was sent to Corona School, in Ikoyi. I remember very little about going to this school, except the school uniforms: the bright red shorts; the red and white, checkered, short-sleeved shirts; and the brown sandals; with white, knee-high socks. These were the days of joviality, reckless fun, and innocent minds. Going to school was such fun, travelling in large state cars and limousines.

We lived in a large state house in Ikoyi, with plenty of space for me to run aimlessly around the estate, playing with my sisters. Being very shy with people, I made very few friends and tended to attach myself to my father, or follow my sisters, who were older than me, around wherever they went. This could be very scary at times, because it meant following them to birthday parties and being pulled by the cheeks by old people, their friends, mums, dads, and other strangers.

I was not always a lively or happy child. Having a hereditary blood disease like Sickle Cell Anaemia left me vulnerable and open to illnesses of all kinds. I was prone to have major crisis, in which my red blood cells, shaped like sickles rather than discs, tend to clog up arteries and veins, creating blood clots. The pain resulting from this can be described as worse than being run over by a double-decker bus, and surviving. Also, due to a low white cell count, and a low immune system, I often developed illnesses, such as pneumonia, and high fevers, but the odd days when I had a mild crisis, I was paralysed with chronic pain from blood clots.

Due to my shyness, I generally used to shuffle shyly around in platform shoes, with a tilted head, and was continuously yelled at to straighten up my posture, for my own good. Now, this could be called *having issues*, but being severely shy was something that could not be helped. I tried keeping to myself a lot of the time. Every time I got in trouble, or yelled at, my head would tilt further, and I would withdraw further into my shell. This, I felt, gradually rectified itself as I grew older.

I grew up in Nigeria, but when I was seven years old, I was asked by my parents if I wanted to go to school in England, and follow my sisters. The alternative was to stay in Nigeria and continue with my schooling at the same school.

I chose to follow my sisters to England, even though it was a different school in a different county. I went to a boarding school in Bristol. That was not what I expected. The school was old, cold, and grey. It was part of an old monastery.

I would have to say, I didn't like one little bit of it. Coming to a new country, from 30 degrees heat down to 2 degrees, I was COLD! I froze to the point of having chilblains and the onset of frostbite. I was bullied senselessly until I found my way around it. I had to stand up for myself, avoid the cold baths and showers, and set a precedent.

To do this, you have to pick a fight with the biggest person you can, and allow them to hit you. This was not as bad as it seems; the view was that you would have to be crazy to pick a fight with that boy, so they would leave you alone.

This went on, and I stayed in my own world as I tinkered with little things, such as toy cars, and on the small mechanical objects, taking them apart and putting them back together— generally, to figure out how they work.

I went to the upper school; academically, I was not entirely successful, as I was continuously distracted by gadgets and mechanical devices. I had to take extra tuition to do O Level maths and English, as the school would let me take the O Level, and just the CSE examination. Once I passed them, I then wasn't allowed to take my A Level choices of Maths, Physics and Chemistry. |They insisted I take up subjects to do with landscape gardening, and called my mum into the school to discuss it. She asked me what I wanted to do, and so I chose to leave the school.

I decided to go to a technical college in Bristol, and chose to do a BTEC in Mechanical Engineering. This allowed me to be more creative and inventive in my work. All I had to do was follow the curriculum, and I was free to do anything else I wanted in the workshops. This was great! I could try out some of my ideas, and if they didn't work, so be it. I was in my element here: no one to tell me that they were wrong, only to assist me when I got stuck. This introduction into the engineering world was where I wanted to be. I finished the course in two years, with distinction, and I was off on the next chapter of my adventure.

University

I went for the interview with Surrey University, and it was a completely different story. They offered support, tuition, and advice. It felt like a place where I really wanted to be. Naturally, I accepted their offer, and off I went. Surrey University, here I come.

My time at Surrey was awesome. I was in my element, studying Mechanical Engineering all day, every day! Looking back on those days, one thing I learned— or came to realise at least— was the cowardliness of racists. It really all comes down to how you deal with this. I found myself having to find my place in the pecking order again, just like at school. But I did have to nip this in the bud. So, I would respond with comments such as, "Oh, crap, I'm black!" or "Watch out, black man's in town!" Mocking myself first took away the opportunity for others to do so, even though they might think you're stark raving mad! But it seemed to have the effect of making the other person seem foolish, and left them humiliated in front of their peers. This seemed to work, in as much as my perpetrators stopped hassling me.

The Surrey Thing

1989: arriving at a new place, with new faces and a new life. I unloaded the taxi, said goodbye to my mother and my brother, and off I went to the mental state of someone who is not aware of what is really happening! I turned around to see this new student step out of an old Citroen BX and struggle with his luggage. We ended up being friends for a long time to come. In fact, he was responsible for swinging me over a wall, and as a result, I broke my left wrist and badly sprained my right. However, I did make him feed me for the next four weeks after it happened.

Now, this was the height of the free Nelson Mandela campaign, of which a lot of new black South African undergraduates came into the university following. I would have to say that this was the first time in my life I had ever experienced reversed racism. Nice people as they were, I was told by some of them, on my second day, that I should stop mixing with *these* people (whites, Asians, and Chinese), and that I should stick to my *own* kind. Well, to say the least, I was shocked.

My immediate reaction to this, however, was to tell them all to go screw themselves. Not very subtle, I know. Well, I would have to say, for the next four/five years, they did not like me. In fact, I later became blackballed from the Afro-Caribbean Society. Like that would upset me! I just thought you didn't need that kind of aggravation. Funnily enough, there was the odd time they came to talk to me…. During holiday periods, when most of them had gone back home, the odd one or two that were left would come and try to make conversation, because they had no one else to talk to. Hypocrites! To be honest, some of the Asians were just the same but not in such an obvious way.

My first year was a massive roller coaster ride. I wasn't like everyone else, fresh out of school, cutting the apron strings of their parents, finding new freedom, getting drunk, and going ballistic. Been there, done it. The awe of the environment, the effort it took to get to that stage, and the pressure and stress of it all, finally got the better of me. For the first time since my childhood, my sickle cell anaemia got the better of me. I became ill time and time again. Firstly, I had a major crisis with a blood clot in my lung, which made it very difficult for me to breathe. I went down to the University Health Centre at around one o'clock in the morning, and before I knew what was really going on, I was rushed to The Royal Surrey County Hospital, and was admitted. At times, the pain was so unbearable that I honestly thought I was going to die. It felt like I was being slowly crushed by a ten ton weight on my chest.

Gradually, I developed clots all over my body, and I was given morphine, its variants, and other hard-core drugs, just to ease the pain. My haemoglobin dropped very low, and my white cell count was so low, I became susceptible to infections; eventually, my doctors made a decision to give me a blood transfusion. Three units of blood—man, I was high as a kite, with a mass fluid changeover. I had visitors coming in and out all the time. Some I couldn't remember, and others, well, they just saw a massive grin on my face. Those drugs were definitely heavy duty. A couple of months later, I was back in hospital with osteomyelitis, a bone infection, in the green line fracture in my wrist that did not heal correctly.

I spent a total of eight weeks, the first year at university, in hospital, and another couple of weeks ill in the health centre. So, I probably missed about a third of my first year, and it came as no real surprise when I was asked to re-sit my first year.

One person that really stuck by me through thick and thin, even though he led me astray, was my mate, Steve. Now, Steve was a six-foot-three rower for the university, and a complete party animal. Steve failed his second year and left Surrey University. He did his industrial year, and then went on to Plymouth University to complete his mechanical engineering degree, in which he got a first. Steve is now my second oldest and closest friend, even though we don't see or speak to each other as often as we used to; but when we do, we can generally tell what each of us is thinking.

Friends came and went throughout my university life, but only a few actually stayed. I always had difficulty talking to people about how I feel, or about my life. I developed a form of a barrier, which always stayed up until I really got to know someone. Most of my friends were women, because they are easier to talk to. Maybe it's because I have two older sisters. This led to me being branded a womanising party animal by the guys. Brain cells... highly overrated.

Being dropped down one year was one of the biggest blows to my ego, and the best thing that could happen. Psychologically, I refused to accept it at first, and I began the year by ignoring the students in my course, and stayed close to the ones in the year above. Most of them were outside the mechanical engineering department, luckily, so we still had things in common. However, as time went on, I gradually had to start talking to my classmates. At first, it wasn't by choice, but at a later date, some of them became very close friends. It sounds a little big-headed, but for some reason, I had hundreds of friends at Surrey University.

Do you remember that Fosters advert in the early nineties, where the guy walks into a bar and everybody knows him, and starts calling out, "Bob!" and waving? Well, funny enough, that happened to me when I walked into the university student union, when I went back for a weekend during my year out. It was really freaky. I walked in and was greeted by so many people; it probably freaked out new students in the union. It really scared me when I tried talking to somebody new, and they generally started up the conversation, after I mentioned my name, by saying, "I've heard all about you." I mean, what the hell did that mean: "I've heard all about you?" Absolute codswallop. That's what it was! Although I did manage to drag it out of a couple of women.

Apparently, I was Mr Party. The all-round party animal, that's me. Wherever there was a party, I was there. Wherever there were gorgeous women, I was there. I must have shagged and dumped so many women; I should have been put out to stud. Allegedly. It got to a point where I just let people believe whatever the hell they wanted. I remember saying this to one girl, and just walked off. She came following me to find out more, and we later became friends. But I did find out who was running around calling me a drunkard womaniser (in a bad way); it was a so-called friend of mine. He was a no-good-for-nothing wanker, who couldn't handle the fact that most women liked everyone else but him. Hell, this a-hole even did the same thing to his cousin. Talk about a two-faced wimp who isn't strong enough to sort his own life out.

Anyway, back to what I was saying. Oh, yeah, it must have been fate to drop down a year. It was probably the reason why I passed. Odd thing to say I know, but it was such an unusual group of people, of which the majority bonded really well together, and the rest went along their own way. Those who bonded well together became a close nit unit, which helped each other, and taught each other their specialist subjects. Because of this, you didn't have to try and learn every subject at once, but step-by-step through others. I was especially thankful of this when I ended up in hospital with pneumonia three weeks before my first set of finals. I had just over a week to cram in all my revision, and if it weren't for these guys and two lecturers, I wouldn't have done it.

The mechanical engineering students of the Class of '94 were known throughout the university as leery piss-heads who party a lot and are always game for a laugh. Most were, but others just stayed in the background. I tended to drift between the two, mainly because I really wanted to keep a low profile at that time. In reality, I had a great time at university, and this is probably where I met a great deal of my friends.

By the time I actually left university and Surrey, my friends dwindled in numbers, and I ended up with just a few, which I could name straight off my head. In fact, they are Miranda (obviously), Steve (of course), Anne (me good mate Oakley), Becky (Steve's wife), Jen and Suzanne (really good friends), Paul (Sue's other half), Lindsey (sensible scatty, extremely reliable and a true friend), Neal and Sam, Ajay, and Cat. I have now known these guys for a fairly long time, and they are the backbone of support in my life. I have a great deal of love, respect, and admiration for these guys.

Continuous Tinkering

All my life, I was said to be a continuous tinkerer. Throughout my upper school, university, and work life, I was always coming up with new ways to do things, trying to *re-invent the wheel*, or make something out of nothing. The purpose of this was to understand how certain things work, and to see if I could find a way to improve that process or operation. Often to no avail. I would continuously sketch things out, but at the end of the day, I would find the logic or theory would collapse before I had finished, or the prototype failed to meet expectations. However, I kept on coming up with new ideas, but nothing really stood the test of time. Nothing lasted more than a month or two before logic took place and I gave up on the idea and abandoned it.

It could be said that I had a restless mind, always thinking about things and never letting it settle. To be honest with you, the truth is that I was never bored because my mind was always preoccupied with thinking of new ways of doing things. In my later teens, I would think to myself, "What if I do things this way?" or "Wouldn't it be better that way?" I would sketch things out in different ways to see how possible it was or how viable it may be. I would always be fiddling and building model aeroplanes or model cars, and making up new games to play, as I spent a lot of time alone. This didn't stop me and, at times, time simply drifted by. Although, in my early years, I was deemed as lazy, in my later years, it was realised that my thinking and restless mind were more at conflict and to do with having a creative and inventive mind, so I was encouraged to simply think more. It is, in fact, the basic start of an entrepreneur mind-set. However, this didn't help when it came to doing exams, as I had the habit of creating my own equations when I didn't know the answer.

This didn't stop me from graduating with a degree in Mechanical Engineering, nor getting a distinction in my Masters in Advanced Manufacturing Methods and Technology. However, I was in my element when I went to work. I could find all the tools I needed to become more creative and inventive.

Lessons Learnt from 1st Job

I thought I had struck it lucky when I landed a position as an industrial engineer with the well-known console and arcade games manufacturer in Wimbledon. How naive and stupid I was. The honeymoon period was soon over. I worked up to 11 hours a day and did everything I could to help and improve processes. This was to no avail. I just got further and further into trouble.

With the excessive hours I kept, and the mass amount of work and supervision I was heavily involved in, I became highly stressed and reclusive. Instinctively, my defences went up. I began losing friends and becoming less communicative to the outside world. After a few months, things became unbearable, to the point of having a crisis and ending up in hospital.

Although employed by the production manager, the MD of the company didn't really want to employ me. Things were OK for the first six months, until my boss, the production manager, broke his back whilst paragliding, and he was an inch away from being paralysed. Then I was made to cover his position, as well as mine. For the next 3 or 4 months, I worked solidly for the company, from 7 in the morning until 11pm. I sacrificed my free time, my girlfriend, and my friends, and I bore the brunt of this. The company employees never understood what pressure I was under when I was running around trying to sort things out.

No matter how much work I did, or how much leadership was shown by me, it was never, ever commended. It got to the stage where I got in trouble continuously with the general manager. He was nothing but a single-minded, brainless bigot, who tried to blame me for his incompetent mistakes. The way I saw it, if they wanted to be sneaky and underhanded, that would be exactly what would happen back to them. When I came out of hospital, I took a couple of days off work, found myself a job, and handed in my resignation. I handed in my resignation and took two weeks of it as my allocated holiday.

This came as a shock to everybody at the time, but I was absolutely fed up with being taken advantage of. I worked my notice period, doing standard hours, and left on good terms.

There were several things I learned from that job. Firstly, you can't let people take advantage of you, because if you give an inch, they will take a mile. Secondly, I would no longer cover for anybody unofficially, because you may not receive any acknowledgement for this. Thirdly, do not do any overtime that you're not paid or appreciated for. Not only that, I lost my girlfriend and some of my friends, and it nearly put me in hospital for exhaustion. This prepared me for anything that was thrown at me in any upcoming jobs. Throughout this whole period, the most classic comments were, "Stress is for whips," and, "We're young, and we feed and thrive on stress." I think these phrases will always stick in my mind. They tend to provide a positive psychological effect whenever things begin to get on top of me.

Corporate Life

The majority of my working life has been spent working in the corporate world, working in and with blue chip companies all over the world. Corporate life was easy at first. I would always get where I wanted as long as I got the job done. However, as time went on, things became hard for me. Firstly, with working for somebody that I didn't respect at all, I found myself engulfed by the workload, and working all hours.

Then, I got smart. I realised that whatever you do, you shouldn't let anybody take advantage of you. In the simplest terms, if you do the work, then nobody can harm you.

I found that concentrating on work keeps the politics away. When people try to do something against you, it falls back on them because they spend more time concentrating on you rather than doing their own job.

I chose my jobs carefully, working for people I could respect, and people who could respect me for the knowledge I have and the ability to do the job correctly; plus, the potential of improving things. There were always people envious of this and wanting the same job, who would do anything to make you look bad.

The fact is that in the corporate world, the biggest game to play is office politics. Offices are rife with politics and gossip about who's doing what and when they do it. That is why the wrong people get promoted, and the right people are left doing the work.

The one thing to do if you are in a threatened position is to stay one or two steps ahead of the people challenging your position. Find out everything you can about the situation, and stay ahead of the situation, and maybe change the game. That way, you will find they are always fighting to keep up.

My career was going well. I had become a manufacturing manager of a specialist metal production, and a lead in the implementation of a new enterprise system, due to the Y2K panic. After the system was up and running for a year or so, they decided to shut my site down. Within a week, I had another job. However, I decided to take a slight turn in my career and work for a consultancy. This job went okay to start with, but then some things happened at work, and then suddenly, things started going wrong. The employees were not treated well. I even got a second warning for being in hospital on a Monday and not informing them. That was crazy!

I left that company within a year and went to work for a company in Royston, doing an implementation there and in Belgium, simultaneously. This was fun, but the company was riddled with people who thrived on playing office politics. I convinced them at the end of the project to make me redundant. I decided to do things on my own and become a freelance JD Edwards consultant. I provided a consulting service to many international companies across Europe, the United States, and the Far East. Providing expert advice in the manufacturing and distribution sector was inspiring and uplifting for me, and it was valuable to my clients.

The Transition

Everything was going well in life. I had moved and gotten married, and work was going well for a few more years. Then, suddenly... Boom! I had a stroke. Everything was turned upside down. I lost the complete use of my right hand, my speech was affected, and I began to slur my words. I spent six months relearning how to write and type again, and to fasten buttons and hold simple objects in my right hand, like a ball or a knife. Working with speech therapists, I spent five months learning how to speak correctly without slurring and mixing up my words.

As you might imagine, this was a particularly taxing time, made worse because I was worrying about my business. My wife and I came up with an idea. What if there was a way to still help my clients—instead of flying around the world to be with them, how else could I deliver to them? Could this be done remotely, or even online? We got our thinking caps on and set about creating niche training programs aimed at users of JD Edwards enterprise resource planning software) who need to plan and execute JDE implementations at large organisations. I began the research, messaged some of my contacts, and crafted the first outline.

Then I had another stroke, 15 months after the first. I had to do something about it. I convinced my hospital doctor to treat me. This worsened the long-term outlook for my condition. This was a serious turn of events, and I had to do something about it. With the support of my family, I convinced my hospital doctor to treat me. Whilst this was a tremendous setback to deal with, my mind was still focused on building an online business. Looking for inspiration of where to even begin with transferring my offline business consultancy online, my wife and I started to plan it out with what (we thought) we knew. Realising we needed to upskill and learn more about starting an online business, we noticed a poster in the *London Underground*, advertising the upcoming London Business Show.

We booked out tickets and off we went to London Olympia. Our aim was to search for advice on setting up a website and what we needed to provide training online and make e-books available to prospects.

We came across a guy named Ian, who had just begun his talk about changing your life and doing things differently. This resonated with me, and as I started to listen more to what he had to say, this only became more appealing. He then started to talk about his mentor, who created multi-million dollar businesses, starting out from humble beginnings in the heart of the East End of London. Much of what Ian said resonated with me, so I signed up to attend a live event to find out more. Ian's mentor is Shaqir Hussyin, and Shaqir is now my mentor. Attending this event was like opening the lid of Pandora's Box— simply put, life changing. Shifting from engineer to entrepreneur, and learning, let's say, the more imprecise world of marketing, was going to be a steep learning curve. After everything I had been through, I felt ready for the challenge.

Now I have three companies to run, and I need to make a success of at least two of them—the original consultancy and the online marketing. I am getting there, with time. Things have been hectic. It has been a major learning curve, but the transition from serving the corporate engineering world to becoming a true entrepreneur and Internet marketer is almost complete, and I am loving my life.

After I came out of hospital, we stepped into another gear and started to make our businesses work. We started to gain momentum in everything we did, and now life is really great!

We have started our business and are determined to succeed at all costs, as we have invested everything into it. My wife is learning the art of copywriting, and I am learning the art of Facebook marketing: the basic and advanced options, and how to get the most out of Facebook (to learn more, see website). The transition from serving the corporate engineering world to becoming a true entrepreneur and Internet marketer is almost complete, and is the main focus of this book. Thanks to the ton of information I have learned from my mentor (who also holds me accountable), I have been gradually able to do this.

Chapter 2

Create the Right Mindset, and Know Your Why

Creating the Correct Mindset

I have always dismissed things like having a positive mindset or having the right mindset to do things, but when I was scheduled to have my stem cell transplant, I decided to try this out for real. They always say you have to go into these things with a positive mind and be as fit as you can be. So, I got fit with the help of a trainer, and went into hospital with an extremely positive mindset. This was so true that the doctors and nurses kept on asking if anything was wrong, and if I was depressed, because people got depressed when in hospital for a long time, especially when going through that procedure. However, I wasn't. I just saw things as obstacles I had to cross over to move on to the next stage, and before I knew it, I was fine, and it was time to go home.

This is when I realised that this positivity and mindset does work. So, I started looking at applying it to everyday life. You can only get a drive to get things done if you have a positive mindset. If you have a negative mindset, it will bring you down to a level of depression, where you would not get things done, and you would rather bury your head in the sand and wish things would go away. However, they never do. They just get worse. A positive mindset will help you take action.

One thing you have to do, if you want to be successful, is to change your mind- set. You have to believe you can do this. You have to think like you are a millionaire, if you want to become one. You have to prepare yourself for everything you are about to receive in your life. It is often said that people have an imprinted amount they aspire to earn in their mind, and whatever happens in their life, that will be all they will earn yearly. So, for example, if your amount is $30,000, you will only ever earn $30,000. So, if you come into some money, you would most likely lose it all, or you will earn nothing the next year, until you go back to earning $30,000.

However, you must readjust you mindset: think big. You have to believe in yourself and your abilities, and above all, think your worth is way beyond your current earnings. If you believe it can happen, it will happen.

The other thing you need is perseverance. All successful people in this game have a lot of perseverance, and have succeeded by focusing on time and energy, and concentrating on learning their craft. Their biggest thing they do is invest in their own education. They learn everything they need to know about the field they go into (Contact me if you want to know more.). If a 19-year-old kid or a 43-year-old truck driver can do it, so can you.

There is one statistic you ought to be aware of, which is that 50% of small businesses fail in the first year, and 95% fail within the first five years. That also applies to online marketing. Over 50% of people fail within 3–6 months, and 95% fail within one or two years. I've seen a lot of people come and go in this business. So, you will have to commit and persevere. Also, bear in mind that the Internet marketing business is not a get-rich-quick scheme. If you want to make it work properly, you would have to put some hard work into it initially. It may take you 5–6 hours a day, for the first few months, to get it going at first.

Having a Millionaire Mindset

Have you ever wondered why some people become wealthy, and some people are destined to have financial difficulties all their lives? Is it due to their education, intelligence, skills, luck, time, contacts, working habits, businesses, or investments? There's one key difference between those who dream of becoming millionaires and those who actually do. It begins and ends with mindset. One significant shift you'll notice, once you follow your passion and are truly operating at a higher level of service to others, is that your big picture vision is as clear as the problem your business solves for people. It then becomes hard to stop yourself going out there and getting things done now.

In 2018, I attended T. Harv Eker's Millionaire Mind Intensive programme, in London. I highly recommend it if you're someone who's serious about changing your life, in terms of gearing up for success, and also to weed out any limiting beliefs about money, wealth, and success. I expect you've heard of this transformational programme. Most people are conditioned from their early years how they feel about wealth, money, and rich people. This may come from parents, teachers, or peers. Things, like "Money doesn't grow on trees," or "Money is the root of all evil," or "I despise rich people; they are all arrogant," become ingrained in your mind. These notions prevent healthy progress and the enjoyment of financial success.

To remove such thoughts, you need to recognise these patterns and beliefs, and retrain your mind to feel positive about wealth, and gratefully accept the gifts from the universe that you attract along your journey. As your mind grows, opens, and expands, positive things happen to you and those around you.

You will have to train your mind to remove such thoughts, and retrain to accept wealth and all good and positive things that will happen to you in the future.

Some tips to gain the millionaire mindset are:

1. You need to focus on what you want, not what you don't want. You have to have clarity of the end result.
2. You have to get yourself a mentor, and hang around like-

minded and inspiring people. (You become whom you associate with.)
3. Treat yourself as a friend. Don't abuse or demoralise yourself.
4. There are no small successes. Celebrate every win, even the small ones.
5. Don't let your ego control you. Trust in your systems and have patience.
6. Stop over-planning; just do. You can waste too much time planning.
7. The only time you grow is when you are uncomfortable.

So, if you want to have a millionaire mindset, you just have to do what rich people do.

The Two Mindsets

Successful people endlessly pursue personal growth and development. A growth mindset is one that believes intelligence can be developed. There is a real desire to learn, embrace challenges, overcome obstacles, see effort as the path to mastery, learn from criticism, and find lessons and inspiration in the success of others. All told, those with a growth mindset reach higher levels of achievement and give a greater sense of free will.

In a fixed mindset, people believe their qualities are fixed traits and cannot change. These people document their intelligence and talents rather than working to develop and improve them. They also believe that talent alone leads to success, and effort is not required.

If a person has a fixed mindset, they are considered unwilling to make any meaningful change in their character. Therefore, their intellectual mind and creative ability is static, and success is the affirmation of that inherited intelligence, an assessment of how those measure up against an equally fixed standard. Striving for success and trying to avoid failure at all costs becomes a way of maintaining a sense of being smart or skilled. However, a growth mindset thrives on challenge, and sees failure not as unintelligence but as a springboard for growth and for stretching their existing abilities. They understand that effort makes them stronger. Therefore, they put in extra time and effort, and that leads to higher achievement.

We develop one of these two mindsets from an early age, and this is what determines our behaviours, relationships, and how we react to change and opportunities in life. However, we can do something to change our behaviours if necessary. For example, to have a successful Internet business, we will require ourselves to have a growth mindset to openly accept new things into our lives.

For example, we will need:

- **Effort** – See effort as a path to mastery, not fruitless, or worse.

- **Challenges** – Embrace all challenges; don't avoid them.

- **Obstacles** – Persist in the face of setbacks; don't avoid all obstacles.

- **Criticism** – Learn from criticism rather than avoiding useful negative feedback.

- **Success of others** – Find lessons and inspiration in the success of others, instead of feeling threatened by the success of others.

These are the things that will help you change your mindset in time, and will help you grow to success. All of these will give a greater sense of free will, and will help you reach a higher level of achievement.

Knowing Your Why

> *"He who has a why can endure any how."*
> – Frederick Nietzsche

If you've ever faced a significant crisis in your life, you'll have experienced the power of purpose to tap reserves of energy, determination, and courage you likely didn't know you had. The power of purpose is similar to the energy of light focused through a magnifying glass. Diffused light has little use, but when its energy is concentrated—as through a magnifying glass—that same light can set fire to paper. Focus its energy even more, as with a laser beam, and it has the power to cut through steel. Likewise, a clear sense of purpose enables you to focus your efforts on what matters most, compelling you to take risks and push forward, regardless of the odds or obstacles.

It is often said that fulfilment is a right and not a privilege. Finding fulfilment in life starts with understanding exactly why we do what we do. Once you understand your why, you are ready to articulate clearly what makes you feel, and to better to understand what drives your behaviour when you are at your natural best. You will be able to make more intentional decisions about your business, your career, and your life. You will be able to then inspire other people to buy from you, work with you, and join your cause.

Your why is the purpose, cause, or belief that inspires you to do something.

For example, what is my why? A couple of years ago, I had a stroke, and was put on blood transfusions weekly. This had a major effect on my business and my work patterns, to the point that I had to take Fridays off every week. I was told this would be for life, until I was referred to Kings College Hospital, and was offered a stem cell transplant. However, this could not happen, because the National Health Authority refused to pay for it. The following year, I had another stroke. It was referred to the Authority again, and yet they refused to pay for it. I had to raise the money and then come up with a proposal to the hospital to do the stem cell transplant, as it was the first in this country.

I could have gone to the U.S. to do it, or to France, but I stayed in the UK, and spent all the money I could earn, borrow, or lay my hands on to have this transplant. My why then became *how to earn money without exerting myself*. I needed to change my life, and then I came across Internet marketing. I also needed a stronger why, so it became *becoming successful, spending less time working and travelling to client sites across the world, and helping others afterwards.* Plus, a vision came to me about a need to build in our hospital to treat people needing stem cell transplants for all kinds of blood diseases. To do this, I would have to become a successful multimillionaire. This is my WHY, and it is strong enough to maintain all the failures and heartaches I could come across, and to continue. Now, what is yours?

We should take a step back and ask ourselves some questions:

- You can start by asking yourself a few of these:
- Why is it that you do what you do?
- What does a great day look like?
- What thrills you about your current job role or career?
- What does success look like beyond the pay check?
- What does real success feel like for you?
- How do you want to feel about your impact on the world when you retire?

You could also ask yourself these follow-up questions:

- What do you hate about your current job role or career?
- Why don't you do something else?
- What does a bad day look like?
- What is it you don't enjoy about your job, and why?
- What does failure look like beyond the pay check?
- What does real failure feel like for you?

Once again, it's essential that you know your professional purpose before you tackle your personal brand. This way, you can discover your why.

Don't ask yourself what the world needs; ask yourself what makes you come alive, then go do that. Because what the world needs is people who have come alive."
– Howard Thurmon

Chapter 3

Getting Started

Choose Your Niche

My niche, incidentally, has always been in the education industry, because I have always educated people in the corporate world, on JD Edwards, manufacturing, inventory, and sales processing. I just expanded that world into the Internet and other business education. To pick the right business to go into, I picked one that resonated with me and what I am doing with my business. However, this was not easy. I had to re-educate myself, learning so many new things, like Facebook, Click Funnels, etc., and how to link them all together, producing new attractive advertising for marketing, creating new dashboards, and running a different kind of business than what I was used to.

Starting a new business, however, is not all easy. Firstly, you would want to select the niche market your business is going to operate within. This can be tricky. You could list all your interests and likes, and come away feeling like you still haven't found your niche. For certain, you would want to do your due diligence in finding the perfect niche for your business, but it is better to get up and running than waste time waiting around. It is better to enter the market sooner, and test out some ideas, and note down your successes and failures. That way, if your first business fails, you can quickly move to the next idea, learning from the previous failures as you go along. Eventually, you will be successful, with a niche that you can grow with.

If you are still stuck or struggling with finding your niche, here are 5 steps that would help you find it:

- **Make a list of your passions and interests**

    You may have already completed this, but if you haven't, make a list of 10 passions and interests you have.

    Business isn't easy; it can test you to the max at times, so why not do something in an area you like. If not, you are potentially going to quit when the going gets really tough. Here are some hints to help you choose your interest or passion areas:

    1. What magazines are you into, or subscribe to? What topic areas do you like?
    2. What clubs or societies are you a member of?
    3. How do you like to spend your free time?
    4. What do you look forward to doing most?

- **Identify problems you can solve**

    Now you are ready to start narrowing down the list you've created. To create a profitable business, you will need to start identifying problems that your potential customers are having, and see if you can come up with a fix for them. If so, note it down. Here are two things you will need to do to identify problems in niches:

    1. Peruse Forums: go to Quora, or forums about your niche, and read the discussions about the problems people are having in that niche.
    2. Have one-on-one conversations or idea-extraction sessions with your target market: Make sure you create a frame work for asking questions that help you collate the main points.

- **Research your competition**

    Competition is not necessarily a bad thing; it just means you have stumbled upon a specific niche. Simply create a spreadsheet and log all the competitors you find in this niche.

    Then figure out whether there is still enough business in this niche so that you can still join, and if there is something that you can offer that smashes your competitors. There are several signs that you can look at that will tell you if you can join this niche and make money:

- Lack of Transparency: many online entrepreneurs have disrupted entire industries by creating a presence where others have been faceless.
- Lack of paid competition: If you've found a keyword that has relatively high search volume but little competition and paid advertising, an opportunity definitely exists for you to upset the market.

- **Low quality content:** If your competition is not providing any good quality content online, or not responding very well, it will be easy to out-rank and out-perform them in that niche, meaning more business for you.

- **Determine the profitable niche**

By now, you should have whittled down your list to a few that you like the look of, and will now have a good idea which niche you would like to go into.

You now need to know what kind of money you could make from the niches you have selected. ClickBank is a great place to start this kind of search.

Browse the top products in your niche, and if nothing comes up, it may be a bad sign that there is not much tackled in that niche.

- **Test your ideas**

    Now you have all the information you need about selecting your niche, and all you have to do is test it out. Pick your product and simply create a landing page, and drive traffic to it.

    If you make no pre-sales, it doesn't mean that the niche is not viable; it may mean that the angle of your message is not quite hitting the mark, so you may need to try another angle.

    Now that you have sorted out a niche, you need to start advertising your products and get your business going.

Invest in Your Education

The difference between successful and unsuccessful people is whether they have invested continually in their education and growth. Successful people realise that the only way to grow is to education oneself and take action, and repeat that circle over and over again.

I find that this is the most effective part, as I educated myself on all parts of the business, and even took up some of the offers I was learning about. But, in the long run, I was able to learn everything I needed to, including learning how to write a book, and advertising on Facebook.

Firstly, you need to create a budget for your education, and save that amount every month. If you need to use more than the allocated budget, you can borrow the money from future deposits, but you have to pay your credit card from the money put in to the education budget. You need to get into the habit of managing this budget in this way, so that it becomes second nature. In general, it is suggested that ten percent of your money should go to your education budget.

If you want to become successful, you need to know that you have to be educated. Ben Franklin once said: *"If you think education is expensive, try ignorance."* Remember, you have to keep educating yourself to grow; if you are not growing, you are dying.

Also, find someone already doing what you want to do, whom you admire. Study what they do, study their marketing, study their copy, study their offers and their products, and everything they do. Model them; don't copy them. What does the website offer customers? Go to one of the events they are hosting. Hang out with successful people. These are the ones who you're going to learn from. See how they interact with their customers; listen to what they say and how they get their message across to others. Watch their body language.

By doing this, you would be able to understand and do what it takes to become successful yourself. You have to educate yourself and become dedicated to do anything it takes to make it. Finally, you will need to constantly have a cutting edge knowledge about your niche, and learn and do everything you can to be more competitive in that market place.

"If you're not willing to learn, no one can help you. If you are determined to learn, no one can stop you."
– Zig Ziglar

Learn About the Industry

Once you've selected your niche, you need to research as much as you can to gain insight and knowledge about the industry you're going into. The quicker you can turn this knowledge into real life experience by doing, you'll become more appealing to prospects, and ultimately successful, because you can demonstrate value into the marketplace.

So, where do you start? You might think you will get a full understanding of the industry from the successes of major influencers or major players in the industry, but to be honest, small businesses (i.e. less than 500 employees) generally don't have the bandwidth to teach you everything you need to know about the industry. They are likely to give you the big picture trend, why their company is disruptive, and where they are planning to make waves.

On the other hand, some small business owners are willing to partner with you and teach you everything they know by offering business investment options, such as affiliate marketing. You grow as they grow. Large business owners are generally inaccessible to the newbie starting out in the online industry, although certainly worth following on Forbes, Entrpreneur.com, LinkedIn, and so on, to tap into their current thinking.

Most searches start on the Internet, so start with a high-level search, and then drill down deeper. For example:

- Top 30 businesses in the opportunity market
- Top 50 products in the education market
- Successful companies in the online education market
- Use websites like ClickBank and WarriorPlus; these provide insight on online education products, and what people are saying about those products.

Time spent on this is worthwhile because it will give you a feel for the market and what is working now, who the masters and experts are in the field, and how much the industry generates in revenue. These are clues to help assess the potential you can tap into.

Once you have done your research, observe the influencers, and sign up to their mailing lists. Look at the email marketing, and read the email content and their offers. How do they write their copy? This is one way you can truly learn about how things are done in the online industry. From their emails, you can glean insights into how it operates and what the pitfalls of the industry are, as well as what mistakes they have made in the past, which will encourage you not to make the same mistakes as they did.

You can also find out what's working now in the industry (and what's not working) through observing affiliates in ClickBank and other places; you tend to get a feel from what they say, how they write, and the buzzwords they use, so that you can copy those buzzwords, copy their methods, and copy those people you most admire in the marketplace. Of course, you need to be mindful to add your own voice into your copywriting. Instead of plagiarising, follow the formula successful online marketers use. Alternatively, consider appointing a mentor who will teach you everything they know about the industry they are in, and who will help you get started and show you how to proceed.

Set Your Budget

Some people go into online businesses without realising or organising the budget required to finance it. The trap some online businesses often fall into is that a lot of emphasis is placed on the products before the realisation hits that there is insufficient budget to adequately advertise and market the product, certainly to start off with. So, you need to make sure you set a big enough marketing budget to start getting yourself known.

"The best advice about money is only 3 words: Get it handled."
– T. Harv Eker

The way to budget is to run your business every month with a clear understanding of having an operating cost (e.g. domains, product creation, website hosting, ClickFunnels), a marketing cost (i.e. advertising costs, Aweber), and a financial cost (i.e. the cost of doing business, such as paying your company's tax).

It can be tricky at first for small businesses to decide how much of their hard-earned cash should be allocated for the Internet marketing budget. The marketing costs on the Internet can be a little overwhelming at first glance, so companies forgo these expenses for DIY Internet marketing. You have to learn how to control your advertising spend on Facebook and Instagram (or any other platform you're using for that matter). Get familiar with the analytics dashboards that these platforms have, because you need to know where your budget is going, how effective the results are, and where best to invest further based on the data presented on the dashboards. The reason for this is so that you can scale up your advertising correctly.

The marking costs should include things like Aweber, ClickFunnels, and all costs related to advertising your products, such as Facebook advertising, banner ads, solo ads, Eventbrite, and so forth. The reason why I say to set a budget is because the cost of some types of advertising tend to run away with you if not controlled tightly. We know that the costs of Internet marketing is expected to rise by approximately nine percent over the next 12 months. This is due to the rise in competition in the market place, due to more and more people coming into that market.

Despite the setting of a budget, you will need to use the budget carefully, and make every dollar go as far as it possibly can. That means you have to have great marketing. Bear these points in mind:

- *Consistency is essential.* Keep your core message the same, whether you are sharing it through email, Facebook or Twitter.
- *Invest in quality.* Your marketing represents your name, brand, values, products, and your services. So, make it count; drive for high standards.
- *Cater to your target audience.* Knowing your audience will determine not only what you share with them but also how you share it. You will need to determine the look of their emails, whether it is mobile or desktop, and structure your newsletters to fit.

Budget to suit, and make this year the best yet.

Test, Fail, Test, Fail, Test, Kaboom

We know that failure in the Internet market is not always failure. In this market, failure is actually when you give up and quit.

When you start off in business, you are not always going to succeed the very first time you launch a product, for a number of reasons, such as:

- Your product may not resonate with your target audience.
- Your ad may not send out the right message.
- You have the wrong target audience.
- There are several other products on the market like it, and you just got it wrong.

Whatever it is, you just have to face the fact that it hasn't worked, and you would just have to make a tweak to the ad or the product, and test it out again. However, it is important that you always keep note of what these changes are that you've made. That way, when you launch another ad, you have a reference point to begin with. This could save you hundreds of dollars, and a lot of time in the long run. If it fails again, repeat the process again, and again, until you either succeed and celebrate, or you call it time on that product and move on with another. Note, this is just the test phase. You have to do this with all products before you launch the really successful products onto the market.

You not only have to test your product, you would also have to test all your marketing choices, whatever it is. You must test, test, and test thoroughly, because if you do, and once you launch your product, then kaboom! The product would be a success.

Chapter 4

Getting a Mentor

Importance of Finding a Mentor

A mentor is there to get you started. In any field that you want to be accomplished in, the mentor is there to kick-start your achievement. We all have dreams and goals in life, but without a mentor, we will struggle to achieve them. Over the past three years, there is one thing I have learnt as an entrepreneur, and that is the importance of getting a mentor. Success often hinges on getting the right advice or support from the right person. This is where a mentor comes in.

At one point in life, we have all had a mentor, whether we have realised it or not. Whether it be your mum, dad, grandparents, a member of your family, or a teacher giving you advice on something, they have possibly been mentoring you.

A mentor can give you a considerable advantage in life, and can have a great impact in your life. A good mentor can offer you advice, and put you in touch with the right people to make your business profitable. When you have a good mentor, you benefit from learning from someone who has already reached the point you are trying to reach yourself. They would understand all the potential pitfalls you could have, and steer you in the right direction to avoid them. A good mentor can help you reach areas you would not necessarily reach on your own, and can give you access to information and tips you may not have access to on your own.

A good mentor would have a considerable impact on your self-confidence if you are having problems about your timing, or suffering from low self-esteem, or you strike out, or are suffering from self-doubt and are questioning everything. You need a mentor with the right mind to talk you through it. When you have a mentor, you will have a resource for life. You will have someone you can ask any work-related question to, and sound out any thoughts or ideas to, at any time in the future, so long as you do not abuse this relationship at any time.

What They Can Do For You

There are several reasons why you would want a mentor and what they can offer you. This is explained in detail below:

- **Look for somebody who has done it before.**
  Their experience can be invaluable to you. There are plenty of people who can talk a good game; however, what you need is somebody who is experienced in the field you're going into. They can make sure you don't fall into the errors they made when developing their business. A good mentor can steer you in the right direction to success.

- **Beware of hidden agendas.**
  Always be aware of the advice you get, and check it out before implementing it. The danger is that they might not be giving you the right advice, because they are thinking of going into the same field that you might be wanting to go into.

- **Find somebody who listens.**
  When looking for a mentor, you want to find somebody that is willing to listen to you and understand your situation before they give advice. There are several people out there who will always be willing to give advice and tell you what to do. However, they don't listen to a word of what you are saying before jumping in with the advice. This is dangerous, as they are at risk of giving you the wrong advice for your situation.

- **Building on your confidence**
  Any time you go on a new path in life, there is always going to be an element of uncertainty along the way. This is always going to knock your confidence a little, but that is okay, because the role of the mentor is to boost your confidence and eliminate uncertainty.

- **Find someone willing to push back against you.**
  If you have a mentor who is always going to agree with you, then you just have a kind person willing to make conversation with you. You should have somebody that is willing to say so when something is wrong, or if they do not

agree with a decision you make. That way, you will have somebody there protecting you from making crucial mistakes.

- **Up-branding**
  A successful association business mentor could help you be up-branded and give the perception of you being more than who you are in the eyes of others.

In basic terms, a mentor is there to facilitate new progress, stop you from making mistakes, and to advise you on how to fast track to success, avoiding the mistakes they made when building up their business.

A Good Mentor

The good mentor never takes their responsibilities as a mentor lightly. They feel invested in the success of their mentees. This requires someone who is knowledgeable, has good communication skills, and possesses the qualities of a good teacher or trainer. A good mentor is committed to help their mentees find success and gratification in their chosen profession. Overall, good mentoring requires powering the mentee to develop their own strengths, beliefs, and personal attributes. A good mentor has the personal attributes it takes to be successful. By showing the mentee what it takes to be productive and successful, they are demonstrating the specific behaviours and actions required to succeed in the field.

Remember, positive attitude must go both ways. It is important that you must treat your mentor with utmost professionalism. A good mentor should always be available to answer any question relevant to the job. Mentor-mentee relationships are a two-way street; consequently, if you want a good relationship with your mentor, become a good mentee. This requires a genuine interest in your mentor, and a willingness to do what it takes to become successful.

1. **Willingness to share knowledge, skills, and expertise**
   A good mentor is willing to teach what he or she knows, and accepts the mentee where they currently are in their professional development. Always take time to stop talking about yourself and ask your mentor how he/she is doing. A good mentor can remember what it was like starting out in the field. The mentor does not take the mentoring relationship lightly, and understands that good mentoring requires time and commitment; they are willing to share information and their ongoing support with the mentee continually.

2. **Takes a personal interest in the mentoring relationship**
   A good mentor does not take his/her responsibility lightly. They feel invested in the success of the mentee. This requires somebody that is knowledgeable and compassionate, and has the attributes of a good teacher or trainer. Excellent communication skills are also required, to give you tips on communication and to avoid the 57 errors you can make.

Overall, good mentoring requires empowering the main student to develop their strengths, beliefs, and personal attributes.

3. **Demonstrate a positive attitude and act as a positive role model**

   Your mentor must exhibit what it takes to be successful in your field. They must be able to show the mentee what it takes to be productive and successful, and demonstrate the ability and behaviours it takes. Remember that positive attitude works both ways. It is important to treat your mentor with the utmost respect and professionalism.

4. **Exhibit enthusiasm in the field**

   The mentor who does not exhibit enthusiasm about his or her job will ultimately not make a good mentor. Enthusiasm is catching; a new employee wants to feel as if their job has meaning, and the potential to create a good life. Your mentor has to take a special interest in helping you build and develop as an executive or business owner.

5. **Ongoing learning and growth in the field**

   Your mentor is in the position to illustrate how the field is growing and changing, and that even after years, there are still things to learn. A person that is stagnant in their field will not make a good mentor. Good mentors are committed and open to experimenting and learning practices that are new to the field. They are excited to share their knowledge with people who are entering the field, and take their role seriously in teaching the knowledge to others. It is important to find someone who is committed to continued learning, and someone who truly believes in the power of continual professional development, regardless of where they are in life.

6. **Sets and meets ongoing professional and personal goals**
   The good mentor continually sets a good example by showing that his/her personal habits are reflected by personal and professional goals and an overall personal success. You're meant to be always busy, and you have to expect that. Make sure you don't abuse that relationship; pick and choose what you are going to ask your mentor.

Finding Your Mentor in Your Niche

Once you have decided on what your niche market is—should it be online marketing, crypto currency, e-commerce, or any other business model—you should find yourself the best mentor you can in that market. This can be done in several ways: searching a directory of mentors, looking at people who influence you, and looking for people who are successful in the marketplace that you can reach.

1. You can search for a mentor in your own group of friends, and see if somebody is good enough to mentor you, through starting your business and advising you to the end when you are successful. The likelihood of finding somebody that can advise you on an online business of that stature is very slim.

2. Finding a mentor from the director of mentors:
   You can scour the Internet, looking for suitable mentors. SCORE, an organization for small business owners, offers advice and mentorship. Simply go to their website, search through their directory, and request to connect with a suitable mentor. You can either chat with one online or find one in your community.

3. Searching your niche:
   One of the best ways of finding your mentor is by studying your niche market. You have to go through the market looking at who is successful in that market, and the successful people who are running courses and workshops, or giving advice to others in the field. If they are, you should contact them and ask them if they could mentor you. Let them know that you admire them, and their success, and ask if they could possibly see their way to mentor you, as you have just started in their market. Be nice and flattered if you can. Once you have your mentor, you should arrange to see them quickly, and perhaps go to one of their workshops to meet them.
   You can always find out who you admire the most, and go to one of their events or summits. Then you can ask them in person if they have a mentorship program, and if they can be your mentor.

Chapter 5

Your Customers

Your customers, especially your established customers, are the lifeblood of the company, so you better learn to appreciate them. Never forget that, and don't try to convince yourself otherwise. If you don't treat your customers well, and appreciate them, then you'll find that you lose them. To be honest, people come when they're invited but only stay when they're appreciated.

You see, all businesses have a front end, where they bring new customers in, and a backend for servicing existing customers with more goods, and they continue to do more business.

The front-end is needed to attract new customers, to replace the old ones that dribble out and are no longer buying from you. No new business can survive without repeat business. The exception might be those on the highway or in malls, where thousands of people pass each day and many never return. The rest depends on people who know them and trust them enough to keep giving them money over the years. Not only do you have to provide a great deal, you will have to make your customer feel very special, so that they come back over and over again. In this section, I will show you how to do this.

Put Yourself in Their Shoes

Understanding your customer in every way possible is the only way to sell to perspective customers. The only way to truly understand your customers is by putting yourself in their shoes, at least mentally. For those who come from the same background, this will be easy. In my case, people know I serve the corporate people who are in their jobs and wanting out, or they have had an illness and are looking for alternative way of making them money with less hours. They are looking for a better life, where they can build their job to fit their lifestyle.

So, put yourself on the other side of the cash register. Think deeply about what your prospects and customers want. Your customer or prospect? What is their gender? What is their average age? Where do they live? How much disposable income do they have in their pockets? What kind of things do they want most, and how efficiently can you get it to them? How long will it be before the novelty wears off, or they have used what you have sold them already, and they need or want something new?

Study your customer base. Do some marketing research based on what you know about your demographics and psychology. Send them out. To serve your customers and prospects (which is the best and most effective way to earn money), you want to find out what they want, and give them exactly that—not what they think they want, or what they should want, but what they really want. As the saying goes, keep your ear to the ground. Listen to what they tell you, but also listen to what they *don't* tell you. Write down everything they tell you they want but don't have, so that you can give it to them next time.

If you can't figure out what they really, really want, then ask them. Politely request some input, or circulate a questionnaire to your existing customers. This is truly easy to do in this day and age, online, and there are so many email mailing poll sites you can use to send your mailing list the questionnaire. Some may answer it but then some may not; either way, you get to know what some of your customers want. Business may be a calculated risk, but there is no place for complacency or guesswork.

Build Relationships

Question: Would you rather buy from someone whom you have bought from before, who you were happy with and had all of your expectations met, and had got a good experience from. Most of us would say yes. That is because those customers have built a little relationship with those shops, so why wouldn't they buy again? The power of building a relationship means that costs doesn't matter as much as trust. Trust is the number one reason why people will stick to one brand. As long as you serve somebody well and keep them happy with excellent customer service and quality products, they will always come back to you.

You will always come across a small percentage of people who always look for a bargain. They are known as the price shoppers, and they typically look for those prices on everything. However, you get what you pay for, because low-priced crap is just that—crap—but they always go through the rigmarole of hunting down the lowest price. However, you shouldn't worry about those bargain hunters; they will always be there, and you can't do anything with them until they come to their senses, which they may. Remember, just try to build a good relationship with your customers.

The real secret to making money is the lifetime value of a customer. A sale may make you a little money, but it's the subsequent sales that generate you real profits. If you can provide products of high standard, there is no reason why your customer wouldn't come back again and again for the next 10, 15, or even 20 years. However, a customer might not stay with you forever. For example, they may die, or move, or even change industries. It is possible that you might have a profitable mutual relationship with your customers until that happens, as they enjoy your goods and services while you increase your income. You will build a core of dedicated customers who will appreciate your efforts on their behalf, as much as you appreciate their business.

One of the key things, while building your relationship, is answering a question that is not clear. Be clear. Very few people answer the question if they are asked, even though most of the time that is when a little goes a long way to helping, and that makes a big impact on the customer. You have to know when to stop selling. People who build relationships know when it's time to have fun, when it's time to be serious, when it's time to be over the top, when it's time to be invisible, or when to take charge and when to follow. Great friendships are hugely beneficial. In time, you can make a real connection with your customer; and in time, you can make a good friendship.

Tell Them Your Story

People buy from people. This is a common saying, but it is so true. My mentor always includes a small bio about himself and where he grew up to become a multi-millionaire. This puts an element of trust in people to get them to buy from him, because they resonated with a part of that story, and want in. Your story can be a powerful way of getting people to buy from you.

For me, I was working for the corporate world, running a successful business, before I had a major stroke, which led to blood transfusions weekly. I then needed to find a way of automating some processes in my business. I started looking into this and came across my mentor, and affiliate marketing. I had another stroke in 2016, and I was told I needed a stem cell transplant. The kicker was that the National Health Authority refused to pay for it. In the meantime, my health and my business really suffered. After 6 months of fighting with them, I convinced the hospital to perform the transplant; and in 2017, they did so. I was remarkably cured and went about building my life and businesses again. Only now, a different way.

The different ways the story is told depends on the product and the circumstances. I tell it because it resonates with my customers and helps them to know me more. It they buy from me, it helps by business and my goals.

With new frontend customers, your story does not matter much because they do not know you yet. It can sway a few people, but you are better off just giving the facts about the offer in an engaging way.

Once you have convinced them to try out your wares, they will want to know more about them, if they like what they see and it interests them. They will be happy to learn even more. In fact, if you excite someone enough—if you turn them into a faithful customer—they will want to know everything about how you got to where you are, because they want to be like you. Once you have a relationship like that solidly in place, do things to strengthen it more. Stay in touch to let them know you haven't fallen off the Earth. Send them special offers, just for existing clients. Give them something for free if you can afford it.

In general, do everything you can to keep your customer relationships strong. Make sure they all enjoy doing business with you.

Thank Your Customers

Grow in to the common procedure of showing gratitude. It will help strengthen your customer relationship, and in the long run, make you more money. As mentioned previously, people go where they are invited but only stay where they are appreciated. People want to feel appreciated, so give them what they what—what they really want. It can be as little as telling them how much you appreciate their purchases, while you fulfil their orders. This tends to work for any business, from the building trade through to the Internet. If we ever find any aliens, or they find us, it'll probably work on them too.

The most successful car salesman, Joe Girard, averaged 6 cars a day. He used to send his customers and staff a birthday card and a Christmas card every year. He had an excellent relationship with every customer of his. He sold 13,001 cars in his career, and he retired at the age of 49. Oh, and he is still alive, at the age of 89.

> *"Kind words can be short and easy to say,*
> *but their echoes are truly endless."*
> – Mother Teresa

Sixty percent of businesses have lost customers because they feel the business is indifferent to them. The easiest way around this, and to make a customer feel valued, is to continually thank them, over and over again, for their business and their loyalty. Through email communications, social messages, and handwritten notes, you can remind customers you are aware of their business and you appreciate it. Trust me, you wouldn't regret it.

Provide Especially Great Customer Service

One thing that separates your business from the thousands of other businesses out there, is if you provide kick-ass, no-nonsense customer service. Remember, if your customer is not happy, they will go elsewhere, and you have lost the revenue of a repeat customer. This can be applied to all businesses, whatever their size. Take Coca-Cola for example; they would go out of their way to resolve an issue. So would Selfridges, Harvey Nichols, etc. Do you know that customer service used to be a foreign idea to most companies? That was especially true to most monopolies, like the old U.S. telephone network, which also served a part of Canada. Despite this, they were losing business in the 1920s, as repairs took forever, and people were waiting up to a year for a new telephone.

Then came the new CEO, who spoke to all his customers and the maintenance staff, and then came up with new procedures. It read: "All new subscribers will have their phones installed within 48 hours, and all new calls will be answered within 12 hours of receiving the call." This made a dramatic change in the way that telecom service operated, and they began receiving new customers when they delivered on time. The reason for this is the dramatic change in their customer service.

Customer service is a pivotal point in your business, to retain existing customers and possibly pull in new customers. Most companies forget who they're there to serve, and that is why they lose customers. So, why are they losing their customers? It is as though the old saying, "The customer is always right," has gone out the window, and many companies are either bored or bothered by their customers. Why don't they realise that without these customers, they will run out of business? They will eventually make no money; the doors will close, and they will possibly become bankrupt. Bear in mind that this is so easy to correct.

Perhaps it is arrogance or superiority over the customer. Whatever it is, it needs to stop.

A lot of the time, customer complaints uncover problems or issues that need to be addressed. Therefore, you must always listen to your customers. Make a decision today that you will treat all your customers well, because great customer service is the cheapest and best marketing tool there is. Of course, truly great customer service delivers above and beyond all expectations. You will be rewarded by this in your business as it excels.

It is true that disgruntled customers will likely be the ones that spread the word about the bad service, so why give only bad customer service? You do so at your own peril. Providing great customer service is easy to do; just be aware, and make it your priority.

There are 10 pillars you need to incorporate within your business to provide a truly great customer service:

1. Be accessible.
2. Listen to what your customers have to say.
3. Respond in a timely manner.
4. Honour your commitments.
5. Never argue with your customers.
6. Treat your customers with respect.
7. Admit when you have made a mistake.
8. Focus on customer relationships—Not Sales!
9. Do what you say!
10. Train your staff.

This does not cost a lot, and it is the greatest key to marketing success.

Chapter 6

Strategy

Never Try to Sell at the Lowest Price

It is generally said that trying to sell goods and services at the lowest price is stupid. Theoretically, it may sound good, but that is why people are always babbling on about matching the lowest cost and so forth, if you could find it.

The thing is, there will always be some nutter out there who would price things below you. And if you react in any way, you could end up in a price war to zero, and you will end up losing as you keep lowering your price. This might be good for the customer at first, but then your quality suffers as you keep getting lower, until everybody loses out and customers stop buying. When customers harass you to keep lowering your prices, hold fast, unless your processes are over-inflated, and you would find, within time, some would sheepishly come back to you.

While it is important to have a unique selling point (USP), never base that on the price. Base the USP on the quality of your products, the quality of your services, the way you have specialised to fit in to your niche, or some other factor. Low prices only work with high volumes, and there are many things that can go wrong and destroy profit margins on even a high-volume business, from natural disasters to bad decisions. Think about it; isn't it easier to sell one $10,000 program than to sell 10,000 one-dollar burgers?

The only way to make money by selling at the lowest price is to sell at high volume and put so much time and effort into the selling that you burn out or break down, and that's when you fail, all at once, even though you've been slowly draining yourself of vitality ever since you jumped on the low-price bandwagon.

You are never going to beat the low price experts, especially the big guys, who would continuously drive the price down until you go out of business or start to raise your price back again. You have to be seriously ruthless with your competitors to stay in business, but you don't want this to become the ruthless tactic they pull on you. Stay away from the low-price war altogether.

Apply the 80/20 Rule

An Italian economist, Vilfredo Pereto, at the turn of the 20th century, observed that 20% of the pea pods in his garden contained 80% of the peas. Later on, studying the distribution of wealth in Italian society, he was surprised to realise that about 80% of the land was owned by only 20% of the population. This later became the Pereto Principle, or more popularly, the 80/20 rule. Ever since then, business people and economists have extended the rule to cover a number of other factors in business life, including work efficiencies, complaints, sales, profits, and much more.

Often, the match isn't quite 80/20. It can be 75/25, or more likely, 90/10. The latter being true for marketing, any marketer or salesperson can tell you that you get most of your sales from a small percentage of your customers, just as you get most of your complaints from a different small percentage of your customers.

For example, 20% of your customers buy 80% of what you sell, while you may get 90% of all your complaints from 10% of your customer base.

While this is a general rule, it still relates to a number of things. Why does this matter, you ask? Because it allows you to maximise your profits by focusing on the people that make you the most amount of money. Everyone else, you can handle on a secondary basis, automate responses to, delegate, or sometimes even ignore. Sometimes the least profitable people or factors eliminate themselves automatically. In the case of large email or direct mail blasts, for example, the people who don't want what you are offering will ignore it.

If you are looking to segment your list, the 80/20 rule can be a good tool to use when you are selling something new and untested, or something you want to maximise your profit from. You simply send the offer to a small percentage of customers who buy from you the most producing 80–90% of your profits, typically; and then, if the offer does well, you can try it with other, less profitable segments of your list.

To summarise this, focus most of your time, money, and energy on the small part of your business that will produce the most profit. You can triage or even delegate the rest, or even sell or give them away to someone willing to dredge the minor profit out of a major mess. Is it a mess you really want to deal with?

Sell to Hot Marketplaces

Stand up and say, "D'oh!" in the words of Homer Simpson! It should be common sense that you have to sell to hot marketplaces if you expect to make piles of money, but common sense isn't so common after all.

There is the thing. Many entrepreneurs start out by having a specific idea that they develop and then fit into an existing market place. The smart ones do their market research first, to make sure the prospects of the marketplace are even interested in their brainstorm. Sometimes they aren't, which causes the smart ones to shy off and try something else. However, the dumb ones, who can be considered very clever in other areas, just carry on developing their products, and are left broke and confused when no one wants it. When you know you can make money selling hand-carved onyx chess sets, or stone pipes, you only experiment with carving stone dolphins or flowers when your income is secure and you have a little spare time.

It is nice to sell what you want to sell, but as mentioned before, you're better off selling what your prospects want. You need to find a hot marketplace and learn how to handle it, or get into a hot marketplace you are already a part of as a consumer; start making contributions that other people want, and adapt when the market place changes. An example of this is Vanilla Ice, the white rapper from the mean streets of Carrolton, Texas. He knew how to take advantage of an existing trend when he jumped on the rap bandwagon in the late 1980s. Obviously, he didn't know how to adapt, unlike Eminem, who is even whiter than Ice, and has been at it for over 20 years now.

You must find a hot marketplace that is full of people and competition; then give people exactly what they want while trying to crush your competition. Be sincere, and adapt with the marketplace. Be Eminem, not Vanilla Ice.

Harness Repeat Behaviour

People in the Internet marketing business often have a saying that is generally adopted: "If it works, do it again." It can be repeated as, "If it works, repeat, repeat!" Take advantage, not only of the repeat behaviour, but also of repeat effectiveness.

Have you ever seen a TV commercial, and realized that some version of it has been running for years, or that they have used the same tagline or slogan forever? In the U.S., Esso/Exon has used the slogan, "Put a tiger in your tank," for decades. Similarly, Kellogg's Frosted Flakes has had Tony the Tiger saying "They're Grrreat!" for a couple of generations now, and Bisto Gravy has always used "Ahh, Bisto" in their adverts. That is because these slogans still work. They draw in new customers on a consistent basis and help these companies sell more to existing customers. Some customers even start looking out for identifiers like the tigers, which is why logos and mascots are so important. The lesson here is to harness repeat behaviour, especially in terms of advertising. If something is still making money, then don't stop doing it. It is more profitable than to spend time, effort, and money coming up with something new, and having to test it out.

You have to milk repeat behaviour for every dollar you can get. This is as true for print advertising, as well as Internet marketing, as it is for anything else. If you follow up on an offer four times and are still making a profit from it, follow up again. If you get up to 10, 15, or 20 follow-ups, and people are still sending you money for your service or product, keep following up, no matter how bored with the advertising you are. It is important to remember that no matter how fast your advertising takes off for your product, it is eventually going to fade, so take advantage of the ups.

However, if you follow up on a profitable offer and you do not break even, drop it. You are done! All it is good for now is recycling into other products, or for use as a bonus or free gift with other offers. If you have trouble pinpointing what makes for a good ad, or an offer that generates repeat behaviour, then find one that someone else has been using for years successfully, whether in your marketplace or not, and study it closely. Reverse-engineer it. Pull it apart and see how it works and is put together. Do this to several, or more, until you can isolate the common factors that keep people coming back. Then you can adapt those factors to your own offers and advertisements to create your own golden goose that lays your golden eggs.

Think Win-Win

There are people in the world who go into business thinking that the object is to fleece the marks for every dollar you can get from them, and damn what they want now or later. Those people are either idiots or con men. With setting ethics aside, you need to look no further than the last sub-chapter to see why this rarely works, unless you are such a good con artist that nobody ever suspects you, or you are always able to get out of town before you get yourself caught.

There should be no setting ethics aside. Professionals depend on their reputations for fair play to keep their business alive and kicking. You are a professional marketer. Although we all have to suffer to an extent under the bad rap that a few bad apples have portrayed us with, you still have to be an upright, moral individual if you are expecting to make a real mark on your field of expertise, and to move forward with your dreams.

You have to construct win-win business strategies and scenarios: relationships where both you and your prospect or customer feel like they have come out ahead. For several decades, economists have talked about how the global marketplace, and human relations in general, become a *zero sum game*, which means, for everyone who wins, someone has to lose. (They don't call it the *Dismal Science* for nothing.) But then again, when everyone is happy, you have a win=win scenario. Your win is that the customer gives you their money because they feel that the value of your offer is greater than the price you are offering, plus they are putting their trust in you to deliver. Their win is that it is a great bargain, something they can either use or ease their pain with, for a relative pittance, or make a whole lot more money than you charged them.

It is important to say that the win-win scenario extends not only to your customers and prospects, but also to your employees, vendors, outsourcers, and others who provide you with valuable services at a good price—people you want to continue doing business with for years to come. It does NOT, however, apply to any other competitors, especially the direct ones! Remember, you are not out to make your competitors happy; you are out to make your customers happy. You should always be thinking win-win.

Chapter 7

Traffic

What is Traffic?

In simplest terms, traffic is just getting people to your website. How you do this can differ in a number of ways. I'll say it again: You build a website; people come to your website. These people are called the *traffic* that comes to your website. However, not all traffic is equal.

Based on the fact that there are many types of traffic sources, bringing in different types of traffic, and often creating different levels of revenue, there so many traffic sources you could use to reach people, if you want to get them to your website or offer. There is free organic traffic, or paid traffic. However, if you want to speed up your progress and ensure that you reach the right audience for your advert, you should use paid traffic.

Your business depends upon the amount of traffic you create, and whether you can build a list of visitors that you can eventually turn into a list of subscribers or customers. This is an important list that you will need to regularly follow up on and treat right. This is crucial, as they could be your future buyers, and ones that could generate thousands of dollars for you. The more traffic you generate, the better position you are to make lots of money. That is as long as you have the right product that people would want to buy (see Product chapter).

The more your list grows, the more chance you will be able to make money, as long as you email them regularly, and as long as you build it the right way. How do you do that? By driving highly targeted traffic to your opt-in pages, which with capture people's names and email addresses. Traffic is the bloodline of the business. The more you get, the more people you get looking at your offers. Mastering this skill could help you to make unlimited profits. I am now going to give you an explanation of a few traffic sources, to get both free and paid/unpaid traffic.

Free Traffic Generation

There are many types of free traffic you can generate, and we are going to discuss a few of them:

Blogging

Blogging is one of the oldest forms of social media; it is short for Weblog, and is basically an online journal or diary that is related to your brand and industry.

Quite simply, a regular blog will help improve your brand awareness, search ranking and web traffic, amongst many other things. The other beauty of blogging is that it is free! Yes, you have to commit a bit of time to it, but essentially, it is a fantastic and free method of marketing your business, products, and services.

You can write a few blogs, and post about your own niche and the products you are promoting. If you've got a few followers, they will get it straight away. However, within time, Google will pick it up and start displaying your blog when someone searches for that product or niche.

The advantage of creating blogs is that you can generate a lot of free traffic to your website or product. However, this is not necessarily the buying traffic you need. The disadvantage of blogs is that there are a lot of bloggers out there. Because of this, you are not necessarily going to start receiving traffic from Google instantly, even though you a writing about your specific niche. This is because there may be 1000s or ever 10000s of websites and blogs already out there, so your blog may be hard to find.

This doesn't mean that blogging doesn't work. It just means that you would have to put a lot of time and effort into writing a lot of posts in your blog to make it work. However, once it starts to work, it is a great tool for generating a lot of free traffic. You just need to be patient and persistent. In time, it could create a lot of traffic for you. You need to have a good posting schedule, and use social media to promote your blog and get some positive social indicators, such as likes, shares, and lots of positive comments about your products. This is a great way of improving the way Google looks at your product, niche, and blogs.

Blogging can take 3–6 months to work properly, so it is a slow process, but it is very good for communicating with existing customers.

Forum posting

You can join forums relating to the niche you wish to go into, and start participating in the discussions within them. You should place your website as part of your signature so that everyone will see it. When you post or comment on any current posts, your signature would be seen. Therefore, a number of people may be curious enough to want to check out your website to see what you do, and possibly buy from you. Forum posting can by extremely powerful for generating traffic to your website, so long as you can respond to posts in a powerful and well-explained manor, putting you in a position of authority. If you can't do that, then don't bother with this method.

Search engine optimisation

Search engine optimisation is the methodology of strategies, techniques, and tactics used to increase the number of visitors to a website by obtaining a higher-ranking placement in the search results of a search engine—Google, Bing, Yahoo, and other search engines. So, if you want your website to reach and show up on the first page of a Google search for the term *Internet Marketing*, you need to carry out some search engine optimisation strategies. Why? Because it is a very large and competitive market, and you need to apply some SEO strategies to illustrate to search engines why your website is the more superior option.

You will need to build a website with the correct structure, and build backlinks (links from other websites pointing to yours), and social links, such as likes, shares, and comments, and do other things to point to your website.

It is important to remember that although the traffic from SEOs are FREE, the fact is that search engine optimisations are very expensive to do.

Social media networking

Any social media site like Twitter, Instagram, LinkedIn, or Facebook can be used to drive traffic to your business, by networking with like-minded people in your niche. Taking Facebook, for example, which is the most commonly used social media site for free traffic generation, you can join a vast number of groups in your niche, and participate in the discussion going on in the groups. Send friend requests to people in the groups, and have a casual chat with them to see if they are interested in what you have to offer. You can also post, on your wall, valuable content, which your friends and followers have the opportunity to comment on.

A question you may ask is, "Does it work?" Yes, and in some cases, very well.

However, even though this kind of traffic is okay, it is very slow to generate, and you don't get enough traffic.

Paid Traffic Generation Strategies

I am going to discuss with you various ways you can advertise with paid generating traffic:

Banner ads

A banner ad is typically a rectangular image advertisement placed on a website, either above, below, or on the sides of the website's main content, and is linked to the advertiser's own website. Not every website partners up with Google/Bing to show ads. Some of the big, high traffic websites prefer to deal directly with the advertiser to negotiate their prices.

To run an ad, you can search the Internet for high traffic websites in your niche, and ask them if they would run a banner ad for you, and then negotiate a price that would suite you needs, or you can look in tools like www.similarweb.com to get the size of the traffic of a website. (The data is not particularly accurate, but it can serve as a good guideline.)

Most websites that allow adverts on their website will have an *Advertise Here* link on their navigation links, which would lead to the data page telling you about the cost of each banner per size, and duration. The cost is per week or per month, but if it works, you can keep renewing it. Banner ads are very good traffic generation tools to use, as long as your image is captivating.

Social media (Facebook, YouTube, Instagram, LinkedIn and Twitter)

Social media sites, like Facebook, YouTube, Instagram, LinkedIn and Twitter, can be used to advertise your website. The biggest of these are Facebook and YouTube, which if used correctly, can help you generate 100–1000+ leads per day, and this can roughly translate to 100–10,000 dollars in revenue per day. The best part of using social media to advertise is that you can start with as little as $5 per day to test out an ad, and if it works, scale it up. If it doesn't work, shut it down and move on to the next. There are two ways of running campaigns on these sites:

Cost-per-click (CPC) bidding means that you pay for each click on your ads. For CPC bidding campaigns, you set a maximum cost-per-click bid—or simply *max. CPC*—that's the highest amount you're willing to pay for a click on your ad (unless you're setting bid adjustments or using enhanced CPC).

- Your *max. CPC* is the most you'll typically be charged for a click, but you'll often be charged less—sometimes much less. That final amount you're charged for a click is called

your *actual CPC*.
- If you enter a max. CPC bid, and someone clicks your ad, that click won't cost you more than the maximum CPC bid amount that you set.
- You'll choose between *manual bidding* (you choose your bid amounts) and *automatic bidding* (let Google set bids to try to get the most clicks within your budget).
- CPC pricing is sometimes known as pay-per-click (PPC).

Cost per thousand (CPM) is a marketing term used to denote the price of 1,000 advertisement impressions on one webpage. If a website publisher charges $2.00 CPM, that means an advertiser must pay $2.00 for every 1,000 impressions of its ad. The "M" in CPM represents the Roman numeral for 1,000.

Free Traffic vs Paid Traffic

We have looked at some different traffic sources, and I bet you are wondering which is best. Even though free traffic can be great, and can produce a great stream of traffic, it is slow, and you need to put in a considerable amount of work to make it happen. On the other hand, paid traffic can get things done far quicker. You know what you are getting and what you are paying for.

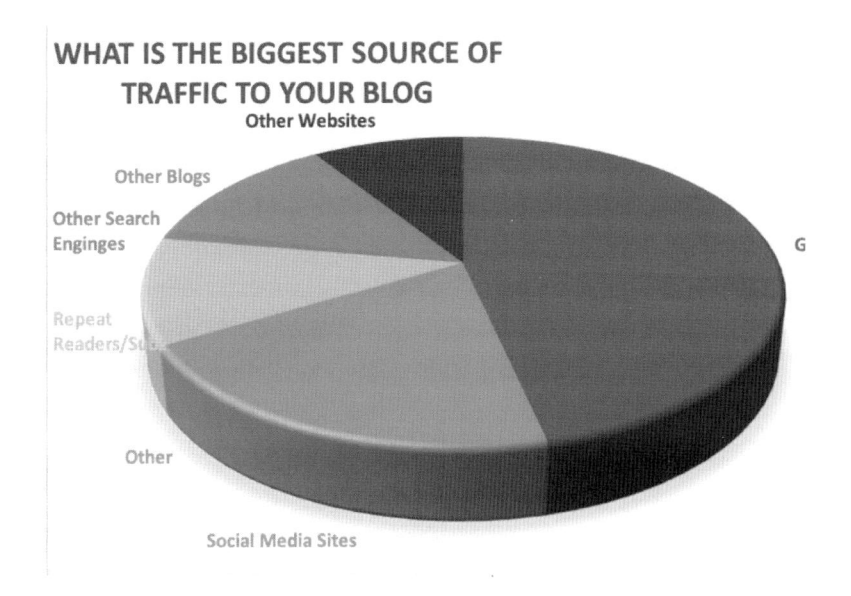

WHAT IS THE BIGGEST SOURCE OF TRAFFIC TO YOUR BLOG

- Other Websites
- Other Blogs
- Other Search Enginges
- Repeat Readers/Su...
- Other
- Social Media Sites
- G

Think about it.

It could take three to six months to build your audience for your website, with free traffic, or it could take three to six days to get the same amount of traffic, using paid traffic. Unlike free traffic, with paid traffic, it is easier to reach your targeted traffic, and one of the main selling points of paid traffic is that you can reach your targeted market effortlessly through specific keywords. However, it may become costly if you monitor your ad spend carefully.

Having understood the differences between the two types of traffic, you may be wondering which is best for your website of offer. Firstly, you have to decide on your budget, and what you want to pay per click. This is a major factor, because if you have no budget, then you will have to go with free traffic, until you can come up the money to be able to do paid traffic.

If you look around and study every business, you will see that they ALL do some kind of paid traffic. This is because you control the game. Converting paid traffic into profit is the ultimate ticket to wealth. Note, if you can learn to bring in far more money into your business than you could ever spend on traffic, you will never have to worry about traffic again.

However, never depend on one traffic method alone if, for example, you have one video running on YouTube that is generating 1000s of traffic to your website, and then, suddenly, YouTube decides for some reason to shut it down. You instantly lose all your traffic in one go; you will no longer get any hits, and your sales will dry. So, master at least one sort of traffic (one at a time), and then you would never run out of traffic. Get yourself involved with more groups and communities, and make your presence known. By doing this, you become a guru and the go-to website.

Traffic You Own – Subscribers

Your subscribers are the most important, because a subscriber is a person that voluntarily said, "I like what you've said and what I've read/bought. I want more." There is no better proof that your content is resonating with someone else in your audience than having someone subscribe to your content on their own accord. To prove that it works, you simply have to monitor your subscriber rate over time, and track what content increases the rate of subscribers the most.

With all that said, the value of your subscriber does and should not end with just one acquisition. You need to use content marketing to put them to work for your brand.

There is an approach you can take:

1. Acquire new subscribers: The audience usually subscribes when they click on the *subscribe* button on the content asset you create.
2. Research the subscribers: This is an important step some marketers fail to do. They usually promote and drive traffic but fail to plan what to do when the audience has been attracted. The solution is to research them. Use tools like Google Analytics Demographics reports, and even events or webinars to find out more about them.
3. Execute on the insights: Use the information to really adapt your business. This could be as simple as optimizing your content to a broader audience, or changing how your advertising works.

Some of the ways to get more subscribers:

Always email your subscribers, over and over again, but don't do it so much that you pressure your subscribers. Provide them with interesting, cool content, over and over again.

Tell a friend and ask her to share. Referrals are a fantastic way to build your base. Remember the saying: If you don't A-S-K, you don't G-E-T. Those three letter words are a powerful way of building your subscribers easily.

Use social media, like Twitter and Facebook. The power of these two social media techniques is very strong. Within them, you should always provide great content, and include a *Subscribe Now* button in your posts. Also, for anybody that asks you questions, you will have to answer them, whatever the question or comment, because all people that comment on your content could be a potential customer or subscriber.

When you have created great content or have come up with a super product that you think everybody will want, don't just sit on it. Promote it, and promote it some more. Get it out there. You will then get more subscribers and customers, and if you promote some other things to them to complement it, they are likely to buy it.

Often, our inboxes are flooded with emails from spam lottery notifications, Candy Crush invites, bitcoin traders, and other spam emails that we completely forgot we subscribed to. But by being creative and being prepared to step outside the box in a way that conveys a clear message about your product or service, you will have effective strategies.

Social Media Example

One example of advertising on social media is Facebook marketing. Whether you are a large corporation or a small biz, Facebook is a powerful marketing tool, and a great place to keep your customers informed, develop brand identity, and broaden your reach.

Facebook is a really good source of paid advertising, which gives you many options to reach millions of people in your niche, restrict the age groups of people that can see your ad, and pinpoint a location by country, or right down to a region in a specific country, like Toronto or Cambridge.

The first thing you would have to do is to distinguish yourself and realise that playing on social media is not the same as running social media or controlling social media. Firstly, you would have to ask yourself a few home truths, about whether it is the right tool for you for your business to advertise on. Within Facebook, you can specify the demographics of the kind of people you want to send your messages to, and you can specify whether you want to send your ad to people with mobiles or people who use desktops to visit Facebook, or both.

The only problem you have is that if not monitored carefully, the cost of placing an ad on Facebook can run away from you fast. You will need to set a budget for your ad, and monitor everything that happens on a daily basis, to make sure all is well. Other than that, it is a great tool to use. (I teach a course on *How* to Do Facebook Marketing*. For details see the book website.) Depending on what you wish to track, (e.g. if you want to track people visiting your sales page to buy) you would copy the Facebook Pixel to your website, and allow Facebook to monitor that action for you. You could also see, from the Facebook dashboard, how many clicks you are getting, the cost per click, the actions people are taking on your site, etc.

If you already have a customer list of emails, you can load that list onto Facebook, and Facebook would go and match the emails with that in Facebook, and you can load that list to Facebook. From that list, you could build a lookalike audience to advertise to. That way, Facebook will only advertise to people like the ones on your original list.

Before you can place any ads, it is advisable to go to the business manager and set up your ad accounts. It is advisable to set up 4 or 5 accounts, in case you do something that Facebook doesn't like, and they shut your account down. You may appeal, but if you lose, you can simply go to the next account and continue placing ads once you set up a credit card. Please note, it is not advisable to set up a credit card until you want to use an account. However, it is not advisable to use the same credit card for duplicate accounts, as they may be shut down as well.

Once you have created that, you will need to start your ad by creating a campaign. You can create a campaign based on what type of ads you want to create, whether it be an ad for brand awareness, engagement ads (getting people to like and comment on your page), lead generations, or conversions. Then go on to set your budget and complete the fields to create your ad. When you create your actual ad, you must have a high-resolution impact image and very good copy to attract people to your ad.

Facebook

Facebook is the main traffic source in which I learnt to promote and advertise products and events effectively. It is a great form of paid advertising, which, if used properly, can help you generate thousands of pounds from your campaigns.

More than 100 million people use Instagram every month across the world, and there are over 1.4 billion active users on Facebook daily. So, you can imagine how easy it is to send out your message to your *would be* audience.

Just one ad campaign could generate you thousands of pounds and hundreds of customers added to your list. All you have to do is place an engaging advert that resonates with the audience you are trying to reach, and you capture these customers.

These customers are yours to sell to, over and over again. You will find that a great deal of them are willing to buy something else from you if the right offer is put to them.

I learnt so many things:

- How to create your own customer audience
- How to create different campaigns
- How to create ad sets
- How to create ads from a fan or business page
- How to create dark ads on their own
- How to control your budget
- How to optimise your ads
- How to analyse your ads

I studied several parts of these paid advertising methods to the degree that I am able to create effective ads, as well as teach this topic to other people as part of my business (See details on my website.).

Chapter 8

Build Your List

The Importance of Having a List

If you are in the Internet marketing business, and you do not have an email list, you might as well be walking around blind. The importance of having an email list is truly essential and cannot be under estimated, as your success in selling products and services depends on it.

Your email list is the bloodline or lifeblood of your online business. It comprises of all the people that have signed up and chosen to be part of one of your promotion campaigns. You have earned their trust through promotions, and they have liked what they saw. Many people don't know how online shopping works, and they have been presented with offers in a specific niche that they can't get anywhere else. Your job is to target these people. They become dependent on your notifications and, in turn, they will buy from you, and refer their friends and family to you.

Your email list usually starts from one's website or blog, or both. Never, ever collect emails other than by asking the surfer directly with the proper buttons and links to push, so that they choose to be opted in. This way, you don't get penalised for spamming people. Besides, you want to get people to choose to be on your list willingly to join the fun. It can be said, the bigger your list of followers, the more money you can make in the back office. You have to remember to consistently feed them with information and be good to them. Regularly contact your list and converse with them. Treat them like your friend, and they will buy from you. Remember, people buy from people, and if they like you and trust you, they will buy from you.

Choosing the Right Software

In business, you can either create your own software to promote and sell, or you can join an affiliate program and promote and sell their products, and gain a commission from that.

Creating your own products, however, takes a long time, and you are waiting several months, or even years, before you can deliver it.

However, you have to careful of which affiliate program you join. There are two main types:

- Low Ticket Offers: deal in selling lower priced products (roughly $1– $199). The problem with this is that they offer very low commission.
- High Ticket Offers: deal in selling high priced products, such as education and consultancy. (roughly $200–$10,000)

You have to ask yourself one question: Would you rather sell $10 products or $1000 products? Just remember that it takes the same amount of effort to do both; so, trust in yourself, and sell HTAMs.

Before you select an affiliate program, check it out first. Ask yourself a number of questions:

- Do you trust the person running the affiliate program? Do some research on them.
- Do they make money from their program?
- Can you make money on that program?
- Do they teach you how it works?
- What is the commission you get from the frontend offer?
- Do you get commission from the backend sales?
- How do you join? Do you have to pay?
- What else do you get for your money?

Whichever product you choose to promote, you have to believe in the product. Get to know the product, get to know the pros and cons of the product, and where to get support for the product, so that if one of your customers ask, you can comfortably answer their question. This may be hard to do, but it must be done to give you an edge on your competitors.

Check out the ClickBank gravity rating, which is based on the number of different affiliates that have made a sale during the week. A high gravity rating means that a number of affiliates are making a lot of money from selling that product.

Check out the sales pages. Low gravity is not necessarily unprofitable—after all, every new product has to start somewhere! However, if a product does have low gravity, then you need to dig a bit further to work out whether it will convert well.

The best way to learn more is to click through to the sales page:

- Check for lengthy sales copy. Short copy doesn't tend to convert well.
- Compare the copy with competing products. Is it convincing? If competitors have better looking and better-sounding sales copy, then there is probably a reason why this product isn't doing well.

The Honey Pot

The sweet spot is developing your list. This is because, as you're starting to gather people's best email addresses to contact them (i.e. the one they actually open!!) with your best content, freebies and offers, you're starting to build a relationship with your prospects. You need to know that the list is about developing a relationship with actual people with actual problems they're looking to solve. They're seeking products and services that will help them resolve these pain points. You will have to listen to them, and ask them questions. They may just be looking at supplementing their income, not replacing it. They may be looking at how to expedite their learning—it could be anything.

So, as they begin to follow you, they get an understanding of how you can help them and who you are as a person. Let them get to know you as the person who can help them. Keep them interested. It's a form of social etiquette. If you think about the same process in the offline world, you most likely wouldn't just walk up to a stranger on the street and offer your product or service to them, thinking that they'd immediately whip out their wallet and buy your stuff! You don't know their need at this time; you don't know if it's relevant for them, and you can't really qualify your prospect. Most importantly, the prospect doesn't know anything about you. You have to build a rapport, provide a context for your offer, and prospects need to be clear on what problem your product/service can help them to address.

Once you have done all the groundwork to provide context and pre-frame your offer, then the list you have been gradually building is warming up to you, and during this process, decides to buy one of your products. The reason your list is the honey pot is because your list is lucrative. Once they know, like, and trust you, they will feel confident doing business with you, and will buy the product or service. Some would even buy all the products and services you have, and ask to work with you for one-to-one consultations, not matter what you charge them.

Writing Emails and Follow-up

Getting people onto your email list is only half the battle. It is important to keep building your list and collecting emails. The thing is, most people only buy between 7 and 21 emails, or longer. That is why it is important to keep emailing them, introducing yourself, and listening to their pains and what they need from you. Then you need to constantly follow up.

There are three words we hear too often and wish we didn't:

- **Just checking in** to see….
- Wanted to **just check in** to hear…
- I thought I'd **just check in** and find out…

These three words are often repetitive and ineffective. We are not "just checking in;" we are trying to achieve something.

There are several reasons why you should be following up on your customers:

People are busy.

Do not be afraid that you might be spamming people. Get that thought out of your head. People have to deal with many different types of emails every day, all of which are fighting for their attention. So, make your emails interesting, and send them out daily. The other reason why you must keep emailing is that people go off on a holiday or are off sick. They can delete a number of emails, but if you have continuously sent them an email, they may get to see just one of them.

People need to hear from you an average of 7 times.

Like I mentioned, another reason to keep following up is that people need to hear from you an average of 7 times before they feel they can buy from you. They may be busy, or they just want to hear more from you before they buy.

You really are leaving money on the table.

It may take months of consistently following up with a client before they decide to buy from you. That is why you need to just follow up. Otherwise, you are simply leaving thousands of pounds on the table.

It is easier to create consistent follow-ups.

With all the automation available nowadays, follow-ups don't need to take a long time to do. These allow the emails to be sent out on time every day.

Automated email marketing can be written and scheduled to be sent out at a certain time of the day, and on a specific day.

Consistent follow-ups will put you ahead of the game.

Most entrepreneurs and marketers give up on their follow-ups quickly. They give up after a few days. However, just remember, always follow up, and don't leave a chance to make money on the table. To sum it all up, don't be afraid to follow up on everything. Never leave money on the table because you are too afraid to follow up.

Chapter 9

Leads and Conversion

Leads

In terms of sales, a lead refers to a contact with a potential customer, also known as a prospect. Leads can be created for purposes such as list building, an e-newsletter list, or for sales leads. A great misconception is that because businesses have a website, they are already generating leads. However, lead generation is actually generating an interest between your customers and potential customers about your services or products, with the goal of increasing sales.

We will be discussing, below, how to generate more interest to your products or services:

Landing pages
Landing pages are a great lead generation technique, and they can be highly customised to the type of consumer that is targeted. For example, an accountancy company targeting small businesses can place a landing page targeting plumbers, and they could have testimonials from plumbers, and examples of what they could do to help plumbers.

SEO

Search engine optimisation is moving your website higher up in the search list. One of the unique benefits of using SEOs as a lead generation technique is that it can actually bring you more qualified leads when done correctly.

Social media lead generation

A lot of businesses are starting to recognise the benefits of social media. However, social media lead generation is not a fast process. Think of Facebook, Twitter, and LinkedIn as different virtual phonebooks that you can actually search by your services or keywords to find people who are already talking about your product or services.

Online PR

If you are looking for a quick way of generating traffic, online ads are a great lead generator for your Internet marketing strategy. You are able to set yourself a monthly budget, monitor your ad performance, and drive traffic to your website.

Blogging

Blogging can act as a great lead generation tool if you are having problems getting visitors to your site, or you are not ranking well on Google. Blogs provide search engines with new content that relates to your industry. Each blog you write not only paints a picture of your business or the types of products you have for Google, but also for your customers and potential customers. A great starting point, as a lead generator, is writing blogs answering questions about your products in an appealing way.

Conversions

Conversions are a marketing tactic that encourages customers to take a specific action. So, take for example, shopping. When people walk into a shop, they come in and browse around. Then they find something they want, and buy it. The process of finding something the customer actually wants, and buying it, is the conversion of a browser to an actual customer.

Driving traffic to your offer page or websites is just not enough. You will need to convert those visitors into customers. That may sound easy to onlookers, but you know first-hand how difficult it is to do. Thankfully, there are tips and advice that can be given to improve your ROI.

There are many different kinds of conversion funnels out there, but they all have the same purpose. That is to guide customers from awareness to taking action. Your funnel has to consist of four steps: awareness, interest, desire, and action. If you understand these phases, you would place yourself in a better position for more sales:

- **Awareness**: The first phase is awareness. When a person becomes aware of your brand, they turn from a consumer

to a potential customer. Your goal then is to instantly move them from awareness to interest.
- **Interest**: During this stage of being interested, you will need to turn that intrigue into desire. This is the hardest step of all, as you have to convince the individual that they actually want your product.
- **Desire**: Once they then desire your product, you will need to give them a reason to purchase the product. This actually depends on things like your price, brand value, and various logistics.
- **Action**: Now you want the consumer to take action. Once the consumer takes action, they become a customer of yours. These are a fraction of the consumers who have come through the awareness funnel.

Tactics to Increase Conversions

When you talk about conversions, you always refer to having a great conversion funnel, but there are also things you can do to increase your conversions:

- **Pay attention to headlines:** One of the first things people see is the headline on the page of your ad. You must take the time to invest in an engaging headline. Focus should be on converting visitors the first time they visit. The battle is getting people engaged straight away.
- **Utilize social media:** Social media is the greatest tool you could use to push potential customers through to your sales conversion funnel. You can get people to follow you on

Twitter, Instagram, Facebook, and Pinterest, slowly nudging them from awareness to action.
- **Invest in crisp copy:** Quality ad copy sells. This cannot be disputed. If you want to sell your products, and increase your conversions, you need to invest in good and compelling content.
- **Give email marketing a chance:** Email marketing is a very valuable tool, with 68% of companies using it saying they have a good ROI. However, remember that the average adult attention span is 8 seconds; so, keep your emails short.
- **Create urgency:** Running low in conversions? Nothing increases activity like a sense of urgency around the purchase decision. Simple things, like telling people, "Sales Only Today," or adding a countdown clock at the checkout of a store online, creates the sense of urgency or shortage, and is enough to spike conversions.
- **Provide directional cues:** People need to be literally directed around a funnel. Using arrows and other directional cues are proven to assist in increasing sales and conversions to product pages.
- **Narrow your focus:** Have you ever thought you are casting your net too wide? You will need to narrow your audience and hone your targeting to a specific niche or group of people.

Planning and Documentation

One of the most important things you need to have in your business is a set of planning and recording to help you plan and record certain things in your business.

Planning

The planning spreadsheets you want are the 30-day planner and the 90-day planner. In the 30-day planner, write down the things you plan to do for the next 30 days, day by day. Decide what actions you are going to take over the next two weeks, and fill in the plan. Then write down your plan of actions for the next two weeks. After you have completed your 30-day plan, go on to the 90-day plan, and continue planning what your aims and your actions in your business are going to be for the next 60 days after. Once you have done this, put it on a wall somewhere in your office, and use it as your plan of action. However, spend 30 to 45 minutes every couple of days reviewing and updating the plan, and keep to the plan of action.

Then, we have a 10x productivity booster.

> *"If you can do it once, you can do it 10x;*
> *if you can do it 10x, you can do it 100x."*
> – Shaqir Hussyin.

It is a 24-hour planner to plan your day, every day, listing your tasks for the day, by time. It allows you to be specific and focused on what you have to do. This will certainly increase your productivity, as long as you give yourself enough time and are truly honest with yourself.

Documentation

It is important to plan and report all the advertising you have done, and their results. This way, you can easily see what is working and what doesn't work, and also how much is costs for every ad, successful or unsuccessful. All your advertising must be documented on a spreadsheet, whether it be a banner ad, a solo ad, a Twitter ad, or a Facebook ad. Log the ad, the ad type, the click, the CTR (click through rate), the CPC (cost per clicks), total cost of the ad, the ad illustration used, the copy reference, and whether the ad was successful, and the number of days the ad ran.

If you keep this information on a spreadsheet, you can instantly see which ads were successful and which ones weren't. That way, you can see what works for you, and you can decide if you wish to repeat anyone of them, or use the same copy or illustration for a different product. It is also a great way to track where your customers come from, and which ad had brought them to you.

Why is documentation important, you ask? I can do it later, you say. Well, think of this... a key employee walks out the door, never to come back, or you step into the road and get hit by a bus... ether way, your business goes into crisis mode and starts fire-fighting. This is because key processes and information are missing. What was said to this customer? What was your last successful ad? Which product are you to promote next? These are the kinds of questions that are likely to be asked, but they can be answered if everything was documented properly.

What else should be documented? Other than what has been discussed before, think about your phone scripts that convert into sales, your upsell process, your policy for handling customer complaints, your process for taking payments from customers, technical codes, etc. Protect yourself, and document everything you can. (Visit the website to see examples of documentation.)

Creatives

One of the most important things that will help with your conversions is to have great creatives. This is striking images and great copy (copy writing).

You will need to have images that are relative to the product or topics you are advertising. The images also need to be striking and interesting to look at, and able to explain what product or service you are selling. It needs to be congruent with the copy and the product or service. But it should not overpower the copy.

You should try and localise your images or use abstract images that would work all over the world. Download the highest resolution images you have, to the ad, even if it makes the ad small. However, try to keep the copy less than 20% of the whole ad.

In terms of copy, it is an art and a skill that must be learnt. If you learn the art of copy, you will be able to write any of your ads professionally, as well being able to position yourself as a highly paid copy writer consultant. Find out what type of copywriter you'd want to become: writing ads, press releases, brochures, or business literature. Use social media to build up a relationship with your audience, via Facebook, Instagram, Twitter, and LinkedIn.

Some of the points you will have to include in your ads when writing them:

- You will have to write a great, striking, and capturing headline that will draw people in to read your ad.
- Make your content as persuasive as it can be.
- Focus on the benefits of the product or service, and describe each benefit that you think deals with a pain point of the customers; answer how the product or service will benefit them.
- Entice the customer with the feature that will benefit them, and provide evidence via testimonials of success.
- Tell the story of one of your customers that have benefited from the product or service, explaining what that benefit was. It might resonate with another potential customer, who may buy, as they wish to get the same outcome.

- Spell out all the benefits your readers will get if they took action, and make it clear and precise what you are saying to them, so that even a child can understand it.
- Ask them a series of questions that they will answer yes to.
- Try and connect to your prospect on a personal level. If you can make a connection with your prospective buyers, you will find they are very likely to buy from you, because people buy from people, not systems.
- Do not make grammatical errors in your copy, as you will be pulled up on it as people spot it.
- Write a compelling call to action. Mention limitations, scarcity, and discounts.
- Deliver the message so that children can understand it.

Chapter 10

Accomplishing Your Goals

When you are creating your business, you have to treat every task as within one big project. Set yours tasks and goals you want to achieve at every point within the business. And it is very important to mark and celebrate each win, each goal, and each success you have within your business, to keep the drive, energy, and momentum flowing in the right direction for success.

Milestones and Goals

Set yourself milestones and several goals within the project. It is important to break down the tasks that need to be done, so that you don't get overwhelmed about how much work there is. Then, if you have a partner, share out the work that needs to be done.

Note: Doing it alone takes a long time. (You first have to register your company. See extras at creativelogicalmind.com.)

It can be said that goals are intentions, purposes, and plans for which you intend to succeed. You set your goals to inspire yourself to further success and achievement, and to measure your progress on worthwhile accomplishments. When goals are written, monitored, and regularly reviewed, they are the most powerful.

You really want to **deeply desire the goal or resolution.** Napoleon Hill, in his landmark book, *Think and Grow Rich*, had it right: *"The starting point of all achievement is desire. Keep this constantly in mind. Weak desires bring weak results, just as a small amount of fire makes a small amount of heat."* So, your first step in goal setting and achieving your dreams is that you've got to really, really want to achieve that goal.

Visualize yourself achieving the goal. Lee Iacocca said, *"The greatest discovery of my generation is that human beings can alter their lives by altering their attitudes of mind."* What will your achievement feel like? How will your life unfold differently as a result? If the goal is a thing, some gurus of goal setting recommend that you keep a picture of the item where you can see it and are reminded of it every day. If you can't picture yourself achieving the goal, chances are, you won't. Make a plan for the path you need to follow to accomplish the goal. Create action steps to follow. Identify a critical path. The critical path defines the key accomplishments along the way, and the most important steps that must happen for the goal to become a reality.

Stephen Covey said, *"All things are created twice. There's a mental or first creation, and a physical or second creation of all* things. You have to make sure that the blueprint, the first creation, is really what you want, that you've thought everything through. Then you put it into bricks and mortar. Each day you go to the construction shed and pull out the blueprint to get marching orders for the day. You begin with the end in mind." He's right.

Commit to achieving the goal by writing down the goal. Lee Iacocca said, *"The discipline of writing something down is the first step toward making it happen."* I agree completely. Write down the plan, the action steps, and the critical path. Somehow, writing down the goal, the plan, and a timeline, sets events in motion that may not have happened otherwise. In my own life, it is as if I am making a deeper commitment to goal accomplishment. I can't fool myself later. The written objective really was the goal.

WIN, WIN, WIN

Going into business can be a long process, especially to make it a successful business. That is why you need to celebrate your successes every time. It is truly important to celebrate every time you complete a task, goal, or milestone. There are several reasons to do this, and some are listed below:

- To learn and adapt
  You need to recognise what is working well, and why, and take something from it to inspire all other actions and goals.

- Develop a successful mindset
  If we decide to change something, whether it be money, health, fitness, romance, or happiness, success is always at the heart of it.

- Motivation
  Motivation is connected to mindset. It is also driven by success. You give yourself many opportunities to be successful. The breakdown of goals, into smaller wins, gives you more accomplishments.
  Celebration gives you more motivation for the next success.

- Feeling good
  The best reason to celebrate your wins is that it feels good. Everyone is motivated to complete because it feels good.

- Happy chemicals
  The reason it feels good, when you celebrate success, is that it releases neuro-happy chemicals in the brain: Dopamine. When released, it makes us happy, and we want more of it.

- Sharing success
  Celebrating success is not always about you. It gives other people a chance to get involved and celebrate with you, and to be motivated and share in your success.

By celebrating your wins, you remain happy and motivated enough to get the next task completed—maybe faster. It does not matter if it is only a small task; as soon as you accomplish it, celebrate! Remember, money attracts money, and success attracts more success.

Who Are You?

Now that we have gone through what it takes to run the business, you have to look at yourself in the mirror and decide for yourself who you are now, and who you want to be in the future, to make your dreams come true. Robert Kiyosaki wrote a book called the *Cash flow Quadrant*, describing in detail how the world of employment and cash flow can be divided into four quadrants.

It can be said to be the best way to become an entrepreneur.

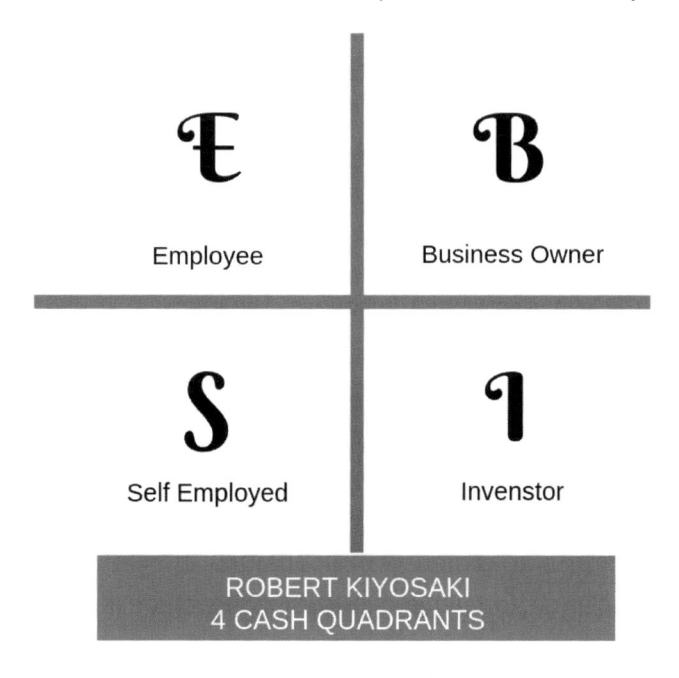

E Employee	**B** Business Owner
S Self Employed	**I** Invenstor

ROBERT KIYOSAKI
4 CASH QUADRANTS

In the business world, there are E's. The E's are the employees, like those in McDonalds or Haliburton, who do shift work or work 9 to 5, and live on a pay check. Employees will always be found saying. "All I want is a secure and stable job with benefits." That's what makes the employees, because their core value is security.

Below that, you have the S's. The S's are the small business owners and the self-employed. Their core value will always have them saying, "If you want to do something right, you have to do it yourself." S means solo. They do everything themselves.

The cash flow quadrant, the right-hand side, contains the B's. The B's mean big business, or Bill Gates. The B's are big businesses that have 500 or more employees. Their words are different. They say, "I'm looking for a good system, good network, and the smartest people to run my company." They don't want to run their companies themselves; they want smart people to run the company and generate the income for them.

The last of the quadrant is the investors. This is where people strive to be. These are people who have their money work for them. The people in the B quadrant have people work hard for them. And the people in the E and S quadrants are the people who work hard for the rich, here on the right side of the cash flow quadrant, for the B's and I's.

The question is, where do you want to be in the next few years? Do you want to own your own business and become an investor? If so, start your own business and get saving.

Mind Your Own Business

We are often programmed to mind everyone else's business but our own. Have you worked hard all your life making other people rich? Most of us are programmed to go to school, get a job, and make money (mainly for other people to become filthy rich). It begins innocently, with words of advice like these:

- Go to school and get good grades so that you can find a safe and secure job that pays well.
- Work hard so you can buy the home of your dreams. After all, your home is an asset and your most important investment.
- "Buy now, pay later." Or, "Low down payment, easy monthly payments." Or, "Come in and save money."

When people often follow up on this advice, they become:

1. Employees, making their bosses and owners rich.
2. Taxpayers, making the government rich.
3. Debtors, making the banks and money lenders rich.
4. Consumers, making many other businesses rich.

INCOME

Income	
You mind your own boss's business	
Expenses	
You mind the government's business via taxes	
With every other expenses, you mind other people's	

BALANCE SHEET

Assets	Liabilities
This is your business	You mind the banker's business

You see, instead of finding their own financial fast track, they are busy helping others find theirs. They spend their lives minding other people's business, instead of their own. By looking at this financial statement, you can see how they have been programmed from an early age to mind other people's business and ignore their own.

Remember, you don't have to be one of those people that spend all their working life with their focus on making other people rich. You can change that focus to yourself, and

Accomplishing Your Goals

concentrate on your own business and making yourself rich and successful. Start first by:

- Filling out your own personal financial statement.
- Setting out financial goals.
    * Create your own 5-year financial plan.
    * Create your own 12-month financial plan.

When you know where you are today, and have created your goals and financial statements, act on them and continuously review them to see if you are on track going forward.